NEW CONCEPTS IN LATINO AMERICAN CULTURES
A Series Edited by Licia Fiol-Matta & José Quiroga

Ciphers of History: Latin American Readings for a Cultural Age
by Enrico Mario Santí

Cosmopolitanisms and Latin America: Against the Destiny of Place
by Jacqueline Loss

Remembering Maternal Bodies: Melancholy in Latina and Latin American Women's Writing
by Benigno Trigo

The Ethics of Latin American Literary Criticism: Reading Otherwise
edited by Erin Graff Zivin

Modernity and the Nation in Mexican Representations of Masculinity: From Sensuality to Bloodshed
by Héctor Domínguez-Ruvalcaba

Forthcoming Titles

White Negritude: Race, Writing, and Brazilian Cultural Identity
by Alexandra Isfahani-Hammond

NEW DIRECTIONS IN LATINO AMERICAN CULTURES
Also Edited by Licia Fiol-Matta & José Quiroga

New York Ricans from the Hip Hop Zone
by Raquel Rivera

The Famous 41: Sexuality and Social Control in Mexico, 1901
edited by Robert McKee Irwin, Edward J. McCaughan, and Michele Rocío Nasser

Velvet Barrios: Popular Culture & Chicana/o Sexualities
edited by Alicia Gaspar de Alba, with a foreword by Tomás Ybarra Frausto

Tongue Ties: Logo-Eroticism in Anglo-Hispanic Literature
by Gustavo Perez-Firmat

Bilingual Games: Some Literary Investigations
edited by Doris Sommer

Jose Martí: An Introduction
by Oscar Montero

New Tendencies in Mexican Art
by Rubén Gallo

The Masters and the Slaves: Plantation Relations and Mestizaje in American Imaginaries
   edited by Alexandra Isfahani-Hammond

The Letter of Violence: Essays on Narrative and Theory
   by Idelber Avelar

Intellectual History of the Caribbean
   by Silvio Torres-Saillant

None of the Above: Contemporary Puerto Rican Cultures and Politics
   edited by Frances Negrón-Muntaner

Forthcoming Titles

Queer Latino Testimonio, Keith Haring, and Juanito Xtravaganza: Hard Tails
   by Arnaldo Cruz-Malavé

Puerto Ricans in America: 30 Years of Activism and Change
   edited by Xavier F. Totti and Félix Matos Rodríguez

Modernity and the Nation in Mexican Representations of Masculinity

From Sensuality to Bloodshed

Héctor Domínguez-Ruvalcaba

First published in 2007 by
PALGRAVE MACMILLAN™
175 Fifth Avenue, New York, N.Y. 10010 and
Houndmills, Basingstoke, Hampshire, England RG21 6XS
Companies and representatives throughout the world.

PALGRAVE MACMILLAN is the global academic imprint of the Palgrave Macmillan division of St. Martin's Press, LLC and of Palgrave Macmillan Ltd. Macmillan® is a registered trademark in the United States, United Kingdom and other countries. Palgrave is a registered trademark in the European Union and other countries.

ISBN-13: 978–0–230–60044–7
ISBN-10: 0–230–60044–1

Library of Congress Cataloging-in-Publication Data

Domínguez-Ruvalcaba, Héctor.
    Modernity and the nation in Mexican representations of masculinity : from sensuality to bloodshed / Héctor Domínguez-Ruvalcaba.
        p. cm. — (New concepts in Latino American cultures)
    Includes bibliographical references and index.
    ISBN 0–230–60044–1
    1. Mexican literature—History and criticism. 2. Masculinity in literature. 3. National characteristics, Mexican, in literature. 4. Violence in literature. 5. Masculinity in motion pictures. 6. Machismo in motion pictures. 7. Motion pictures--Mexico. I. Title.

PQ7122.M37D66 2007
860.9'353—dc22   2007011886

A catalogue record for this book is available from the British Library.

Design by Newgen Imaging Systems (P) Ltd., Chennai, India.

First edition: November 2007

10 9 8 7 6 5 4 3 2 1

Printed in the United States of America.

Contents

Acknowledgments

The writing of this book was made possible by the sponsorship of Denison University, The University of Texas at Austin, the Sherman Fairchild Foundation, and the Title VI Professional Development Grant. I am especially thankful for the generous support of Professor Leopoldo Bernucci and Professor Nicolas Shumway.

I am indebted to Professor Ileana Rodríguez, Professor Emilio Bejel, and Professor Jossianna Arroyo-Martínez, for their meticulous reading and suggestions. I want also to express my gratitude for the help and patience of my editors Judith Rosenberg, Elizabeth Washington and Joseph Pierce, who offered detailed and invaluable advice for rewriting my manuscript. I also want to acknowledge the invaluable support of all my colleagues in Denison University and The University of Texas at Austin. Finally, I thank my friends Patricia Ravelo, Rossina Conde, James Harrington, Óscar Sánchez, and Arturo Benjamín Pérez for always being there.

Note: All translations in the book are mine.

I

Introduction

The objective of this book is to study the relevance of masculinity in Mexican culture. To achieve this goal I propose to interpret male representation as intersected or mediated by the historical process that constitutes the narrative of the nation in the modern period. I offer a theory of maleness not as the knowledge of the male body itself, but as a description of the historical, social, political, religious, and cognitive contexts that enable our perception of it. As Susan Bordo asserts, "[T]he body doesn't carry only DNA, it also carries human history with it" (26). Thus the density of masculinity is based on its semiotic magnitude. Masculinity as a gender category is culturally produced not only as a perceived entity but also as a device for perception. It is a means by which we can know the peculiarities of a nation's culture. We talk about masculinity, not only as a problem of gender, but also as a problem of knowledge that the masculine figure poses. Although the term "masculine" depends semantically on its differentiation from the term "feminine"—which reduces its conception to a binary sexual paradigm—its representation appears related to a broader symbolic universe: maleness participates in a rhetorical operation in which it allegorizes historical entities such as nation, modernity, and colonialism or functions as a metonym—relationships of cause-effect, container-content, fraction-wholeness—of social phenomena such as work, violence, oppression, and resistance.

I depart from the assumption that the politics of art production and reception is defined by a gender system whose structure of differences articulates the uses of representations. My endeavor in this book is to show not only how modern Mexican culture, as in all Western civilization, is built on a structure of gender and patriarchy, , but also how this modern masculinity, although connected in general terms to the Western gender principles, has specific features that have resulted from colonial and postcolonial processes. This book does not just point out nuances between the ruling imperialism and its dependent cultures. As its title indicates, it is also concerned with the deep contradictions expressed in the linkage between sensuality and violence. Modern civilization proposes sensuality and provokes violence. The journey from sensuality to violence is the plot of my book, which is based on four arguments I summarize in the pages that follow.

1. Representation of masculinity is an allegory of the nation, but this allegory can be conceived only through paradoxes.

My review of how the male is imagined focuses on the interstices and paradoxes that flow from this allegory. My goal is to underscore those moments of Mexican culture between the Porfiriato (1876–1911) and the first years of the twenty-first century, in which the hegemony of the masculine is put into question. Here we find the signs that point to the profile of the community-nation, its norms, and its limits. This symbolic systematization can be defined, according to Elsa Muñiz, as a civilizing process based on the differences of social functions reinforced by institutions and strict mechanisms of surveillance intended to keep intact the notions of femaleness and maleness (Muñiz 8). The middle-class formation that Muñiz addresses emphasizes the gender system of the Porfiriato and the postrevolutionary period. Against this background and within this collectivity, I propose to highlight the zones of exclusion. I intend to shed light on the hidden aspects of masculine representation—the scandals, the prejudices, the permissive areas, and the strategies of segregation: in sum, all aspects that conservative middle-class "civilization" tends to make invisible. Repression, punishment, and morbid curiosity are instruments of power that pervade a broad production of images and discourses. As Robert Buffington observes when discussing depictions of transvestitism in newspaper cartoons during the Porfiriato, politics is sexualized through homophobia (199). Carlos Monsiváis asserts that the scandal disseminated around the 1901 case of the transvestites' ball of the "41" proves the recognition of the existence of homosexuality (1998: 2,18). In Martín Luis Guzmán's narratives and Ismael Rodríguez's films, homosociety defines an attraction from male to male. In Hugo Argüelles' theater, in Luis Zapata's novel, and in ethnographies on popular homosexuality, we find that homoeroticism and machismo are not opposed but intersect in the characterization of male sexuality. In these works, satire, attraction, and scandal open the way to a chain of rhetorical processes that destabilizes social discourses. The materials that I examine in this book underline the signifying character of gender transgression and its political materialization in the public sphere. Representations of the transgressing body unleash a struggle expressed through phobias and seductions that penetrates beyond sexuality into all dimensions of daily life.

2. Mexican masculinity is an invention of modern colonialism, in which sensualizing means disempowerment.

This book is an attempt to understand how modernity, nation, and masculinity intersect in the representation of men. Modernity is a project imposed by a paternalist conception of government in all historical periods (the 1870s to the 2000s) my analysis covers. Instead of offering a way for the development of democratic society, modern paternalism reproduces the colonial dependency model in which the national is fatally fixed in the subaltern position of unending subjugation to an influx of external civilizing influences. This authoritarian modernity reveals that maleness, as allegorical resource of the nation, is a central trope for understanding Mexican culture. However, this Mexican maleness, which locates the representation of the national in spontaneity instead of making it a deliberate project of the nation, is more natural than rational, more impulsive than controlling.

Sensualizing of the male body amounts to derationalizing the masculine and derogating one of the main attributes of masculinity in Western culture since the Enlightenment, according to Victor J. Seidler (14); but, sensualizing of men also implies their disempowerment and their representation as subjects who cannot control their own impulses. Sensuality reflects the perception of colonized maleness as lacking reason and power and being ruled by emotions. Mexican naturalism and the representation of the indigenous population in the beginning of the twentieth century support the argument that modernity in the arts proposes sensualization of the Mexican male as a symbolic strategy for disempowering him. By the same token, representation of machos in classic cinema configures a melodramatic exaltation of national masculinity.

The idea of disempowering through sensuality leads to the deconstruction of virility through transvestism. Political cartoons of the nineteenth century reiterate the definition of power as virility, and effeminacy as antinational representation. Effeminacy constitutes a device for emasculating political enemies—whereas the military and *charro* (Mexican cowboy) garment denote empowerment. Embodying the image of the excluded, the effeminate male appears repeatedly throughout the twentieth century as confirmation that the excluded is actually an integral part of the disputes that form the national imaginary. Yet, as is shown in several instances, the excluded feminine and effeminate figures form the cornerstone on which the masculine hegemony rests: the case of the forty-one ball in 1901, the derogatory statements against effeminate intellectuals in the postrevolutionary period, and the contemporary murders of women and homosexuals are some of the cases this book discusses in this regard. By focusing on phobias to apprehend masculinity, we take a negative perspective: the masculine is known by what it rejects. This position

leads to an exposé of the contradictions of the patriarchy. The understanding
of the masculine hegemony is necessarily an understanding of the politics it
performs. In these relationships the moral and aesthetic determinations of the
masculine reveal a system of phobias and desires that maps out a vertiginous
route of rejections and attractions that constitute male representation.

3. The Mexican state has a homosocial feature, and homosociety is shaped
by misogyny and homophobia.

One of the central statements of this book is that homosocial bonds
characterize the Mexican political structure. If the male hegemony is produced
by phobias, we must question the analogy between homosociety and the state.
While misogyny and homophobia construct national otherness, heterosexual
masculinity occupies the center stage, that is, the collective's desirable self, represented as the homosocial gathering of men. Homosociety and homophobia
are the two faces of Mexican masculinity. The former corresponds to the
desirable man and the latter to his rejection. The two depend on each other, to
nurture the content of moral structures and to generate rationales and
simulacra of sense to confirm the necessity for patriarchy.

Homosociety prevails as a principle of social cohesion despite revolutions
and postmodernity: this is the main assumption that provides coherence to the
hegemony of masculinity throughout modern history. The structure in which
the patriarchal hegemony in Mexico is rooted consists of three versions of
homosociety: the belief in the totalitarian state associated with the modernization of the Porfiriato, the belief in the paternalism of the postrevolutionary
state, and the belief in the violence of postmodern times. In this sense,
homosociety is the model for the Mexican state. Masonic loggias, the revolutionary elite, recreational and economic activities, all gather males and thus
political, social, economic, and cultural life are structured around men.

The monumental cult of the image of male heroes as a central reference in
the syntax of the city requires an explanation. Staged at the point of conver-
gence of streets, and occupying the pinnacle of public space, the images of
male heroes constitute a statement of masculine supremacy. Here are staged
the ideas of state and power, and all the abstractions that symbolize the
nation. Through this monolithic representation, from the most elevated public image to the most intimate and disdained representations, the male body
reveals, not the Habermasian scheme of the ideal rational state, but the
dynamics of fluxes and excretions, the currents of communicative actions that
configure the fiction of the nation, as well as the failures and compulsions of
the representations.

An analysis of the masculine is incomplete without a consideration of the
relationship between gender categories. This relationship involves the conflictive contacts that the patriarchal system imposes through its hierarchical structure. The conflictive—often violent—contact between gender categories enables
the construction of alternative identities, mainly through two mechanisms of
exclusion: homophobia and misogyny. Literature and the arts in general again

and again show this negative relationship. However, this work, instead of dealing with the binary extrapolation of the oppressive patriarchy and the oppressed marginal, studies the internal contradictions in homophobic and misogynist bias.

The border between hate and desire outlines power relations. In this regard, I propose gender as the criterion for the analysis of the state, specifically, homosocial hegemony and its misogynist and homophobic politics, which is defined in terms of desire and phobia. In the politics of desire and phobia, meaning is not produced through the execution of concepts; rather it depends on the positions its enunciation takes. Here it is important to locate the subject who represents (who has the agency that generates the representation), the object represented (either the object of desire or its rejection), and the addressee for whom representation is performed, where the phobia or desire is perceived, disseminated, mythologized, and deconstructed.

The relationship between desire and hate is dialectic, never a definite opposition. Homophobia and male-to-male attraction appear interrelated in narratives of homosociety. As in the machinery of Deleuze and Guattari, a system of fluxes of desire results in a system of excretions, or vice versa (11–17). If homosocial politics is characterized as a process of fluxes and expulsions, when we discuss masculinity as a metaphor for the nation, rather than as the imagined community proposed by Benedict Anderson, we could suggest that the nation represented is a compulsive oscillation between desire and expulsion, acceptance and rejection. Phobias and desires, therefore, make misogyny and homophobia constitutive for the representation of the nation.

My critique of homosociety requires the detachment of desire from hegemonic interest (which here is interpreted as the patriarchal, modern, and national ordering of the field of desire), and the discovery in its representations of the traces of their deconstruction. This will mean the deconstruction of the machinery that determined desirable images, which will lead us to reconsider the representation of males as the representation of disputed meanings. As contradictory, conflicting, or disputed as this work is, it still comprehends the Mexican masculinity as the battlefield of signification, where misogyny and homophobia are not just forms of domination and machismo, but also the fissures that enable its deconstruction.

4. Machismo is an epistemological instrument for critiquing both the state and violence.

Writers, ethnographers, artists, and academics who inquire into the currents of compulsions and failures argue that Mexican machismo depends on the contradictions of ethnicity and nationality in the context of modernity. Imagining and knowing Mexican masculinity in the symbolic fields of the nationality-colonialism dyad makes possible the characterizations that nurture the narratives of fiction, art, films, chronicles, and so on. Rancor, inferiority, hedonism, fear, ritualized challenge, fatality, seduction, and double standards are terms that refer to the drama of colonization or to the illusions of modernity expressed in the representations of men. Most discourses on the masculine are articulated in a negative mode. Masculine desire bears a destructive effect. Violent eroticism is found in the nineteenth century fin de siècle art and literature, in the novel of revolution, and in classical and contemporary popular films. It is reflected in the essayist tradition on Mexicanness, which began in the 1930s. It is the theoretical ground of most ethnographies on Mexican society. Intellectual interventions throughout the twentieth century problematize masculine desire, resulting in a problematization of the symbolical order of the nation. Critical thought singles out desire, abjection, and ambiguities to characterize the specificity of the national. Terms such as traumas, scars, resentment, and guilt show that the pathology of the macho generates the failure of modernization.

I try to explain how the structure of the norms of social behavior that define and control bodies in Mexican machista society authorizes the community to exclude, condemn, discriminate against, and coerce those whom the patriarchy defines as its others. I also try to show how these excluded bodies interfere with the social norm, which is indeed a mechanism of production of physical and symbolic violence, as it mandates the control, punishment, and persecution of strange bodies. My critical intervention is devoted to emphasizing the strategies of domination through which the hegemony becomes hegemonic, while revealing the mechanisms of simulation and evidencing the incoherence of the social law. In this sense, my analysis is intended to dismount the moral and aesthetic machinery that organize masculinity. This skepticism of mine should be understood as a methodological tactic, a way to escape from the dominance of the patriarchy as a first step toward disempowering it, that is, to deauthorize the violence that the text of social law enables and provokes.

If we identify patriarchal law with violence, rather than recognize its effectiveness in the construction of social order, it is because in gender and sexual matters, national culture has revealed, especially in the last decade of the twentieth century and the beginning of the twenty-first, a compulsion for immolating women and homosexuals. On the one hand, we have the ever-growing movements concerning women and sexual diversities, which have, since the beginning of the twentieth century, significantly influenced literature, art, media, education, and political agendas; on the other, we still have sectors of the state and civil society (from churches to political and criminal organizations) that reinforce patriarchal institutions such as the family, homosocial spaces, and heterosexuality, and create a climate of impunity and complicity with the sacrifice of subaltern bodies. This violence needs an urgent study.

I argue in this work that the state of terror and inequality that characterizes masculine dominance in Mexico is based on a politics of desire. Desire is the foundation of gender; its principle is relational, and it is articulated in terms of the machinery of social goods. Social prestige acquired through valuable masculine attributes is among the most appreciated of social goods. The politics of desire converts the reasons for excluding bodies into valuable attributes. The system of desire is historical; it functions in the ethic and aesthetic spaces. A reflection on desire is an exercise in deconstruction that deals with the assumptions of what is desirable in both moral rationality and artistic intuitions.

The key concepts of this book are homophobia, misogyny, and homosociety, which are understood as the constitutive axes of machismo and peripheral (colonized) modern culture. My endeavor is to explore instances of discursive and visual materials in which we can find the places and mechanisms that articulate masculinity. I seek to put forward a practical theory of desire that converts aesthetic expression into ethical reflection. Mine is a study of the political meaning of maleness; that is, we try to understand the process that makes the masculine a significant entity. Here man is presented to our gaze both as its exterior expression and its fissures; here I confront what hegemonic masculinity claims to be and its deadening silence in order to offer a reflection on the linkage between intimacy and coercion and their implications for the concept of nation.

Part I

Sensual Interventions

2

Sense of Sensuality

This chapter focuses on the representation of the male body in the art and literature of the last decades of the nineteenth century and the beginning of the twentieth century. It aims to answer the question: How is maleness produced as part of the project of modernization in Mexican arts? Departing from a reflection on the meaning of sensuality in this period, I argue that the aesthetics of modern masculinity in Mexico must be understood in the context of colonialism—as modernity perpetuates the cultural dependency of the colonized on their erstwhile colonizers. On the basis of the sculptures of the heroes as well as the depiction of male sensuality in art and narrative and the depiction of Mexican Indians and mestizos in painting, this chapter argues that the male body offers the keys for understanding the process of modernization in Mexico. First, we find in the nudist art of the Academia de San Carlos a pleasurable representation of men, in contrast with the symbolical representation of romantic heroes one generally comes across in most art forms. Second, in the depiction of the sexual nature of men in naturalist stories, it is possible to trace a way of fighting traditional contention of the body longing in naturalist narrative. Third, representation of Indians and mestizos in this period shows the westernization of the natives by providing them with sensuality and subjectivity, so that they can be read in the modern code. These then are three aspects of male body representation in which sensuality and colonialism intersect.

Enjoyable Males

In a speech delivered in 1873 during an awards ceremony at the Academia de San Carlos art school, D. Pelegrín Clavé, the director of painting, regretted that art had become sensual, as the cult of form replaced Christian inspiration (Romero de Terreros 354). The cult of form, linked to sensuality in Pelegrín's speech, expresses a new direction of art in fin de siècle modernity; characteristically it focuses on representation of the body. In the works of the Academia that Pelegrín refers to, the object of art becomes a domain of senses. Sensuality in art gratifies the senses by means of perception. Then sensuality, that is, the pleasurable depiction of the body, inserts itself as the content of art works. The body itself implies its intrinsic meaning through the suppression of any extrabody content in the artistic appreciation. That is, nude representation in the works at the Academia de San Carlos proposes that art value is implicit in the beauty of the human body, and there is nothing to see beyond its surface. Conceptualization of beauty refers only to the body form. It is a discourse that invisibly dresses the body and prevents the gaze from being distracted by any interest other than the enjoyment of bodies. Sensuality consists of the body as an object of beauty.

The use of body as an aesthetic norm is part of the taste of _modernismo_.[1] Sensuality conveys hedonism, and hedonism is manifested in the field of sensations. Christianity and the nation, the concepts that were used to determine art production and reception in the earlier artistic periods, lost their influence in the second half of the nineteenth century in Mexico. The triumph of the Republic against French intervention in 1867 is also the triumph of the liberal bourgeoisie and the start of a new colonialism based on liberalization of markets modeled on British free-trade politics. This geopolitical context locates Mexico in the cartography of the movement of merchandise and discourses that define modernity: that process of urbanization and divulgence, devolution, distribution, and vulgarization of ideas, which challenges the two systems of homogeneity: the Catholic Church that the Reform laws (1857) of liberal politicians such as Benito Juárez and Miguel Lerdo de Tejada constrained politically; and the romantic nationalism that cohabits with cosmopolitan forms of life. In modernity, art tends to be private, to give pleasure, and to find its own meaning in sensuality. If sensuality is the subject of sculpture by Enrique Guerra, Fidencio Nava, and Agustín Campos (Velázquez 24), who were influential in the last decade of the nineteenth century, we have to agree that sensuality is based on the enjoyment of the gaze and that it detaches reception from Christian and national conceptualizations.

A field of meaning coterminous with the senses, sensuality connotes the resistance to the Christian and nationalist rituals. The immediate reference to sensory experiences keeps sensuality descriptive and on the surface. *Modernista* art introduces appearance, in and of itself, in contrast with the symbolic constructions of iconography in the romantic and baroque periods, which depended on codifications beyond the image as a condition of intelligibility.

Besides *modernista* art, from independence to the postrevolutionary period, masculine bodies in nationalistic paintings were dressed with allegorical codes. Men were represented by the heroic body: dominance, decision, and sacrifice characterized the body in romantic painting, in monuments erected during the Porfiariato, and in postrevolutionary muralism. Emblems, standards, uniforms, and coats-of-arms determined the male bodies' meaning, while written objects such as books, documents, and banners prevented the work from being misinterpreted. The content of these pieces is a series of visual commands and a litany of symbolic paraphernalia that makes art a public–political activity. Military governments imposed a form of figurative expression, making the images of males narrate the country's mythology. In the exhibition "La Contrucción del Estado" [The Construction of the State] in the fall of 2003, in the Museo Nacional de Arte in Mexico City, the protagonists of national narratives are presented in their most public tasks: they celebrate agreements, play at or enact ceremonies of surrendering, founding of towns and buildings, entering the city celebrating triumph, performing military feats, or retiring from the battlefield after defeat. During the Porfiriato, statues of the builders of the nation placed along Paseo de la Reforma Avenue in Mexico City carry out this representative articulation of the patriarchal nation. In the last decades of the nineteenth century, the state sponsored projects, such as the Cuauhtémoc and Juárez monuments by Miguel Noreña, to honor its heroes. For the celebration of the centenary of the Hidalgo's insurrection, the monument to the independence was erected. Thus the nation is depicted through its male bodies. Depictions of males in romanticism were clearly equivalent to the national saga; hence male bodies take their place in the system of icons that serve the national project. Male bodies depend on this nationalist discourse in order to signify as the bodies of the heroes. *Modernista* art proposes, in contrast, to focus the gaze on the bodily form—without dress. By conceiving of a gaze that grounds or concretizes perception through a process of objectification and furthermore goes on to construct subjectivity, my point of departure is to propose the gaze as a mechanism that constitutes a system of meanings and symbolic valences beyond dress, in short, a cultural universe in which we experience the *sense* of body itself. In my usage *sense* and experience are synonyms; *sense* refers to a coherent continuum of meaning and *experience* includes a series of events in a meaningful process; at the same time, however, the terms retain a tension between mental and sensory processes of knowing, a dissonance that discomforts the ambivalent phases of *modernismo*. *Modernista* narrative and painting draw the image of modernity through this ambivalence; such is the formalization of that cultural scene.[2] How does the masculine body take its place, or makes sense, in this scenerio? What are its principles of codification? The modern masculine body is codified in the context of a peripheral modernity. The term "peripheral modernity" used by Beatriz Sarlo to refer to the coexistence of residual and defensive elements, and innovative programs at the beginning of the twentieth century in Buenos Aires, can be applied to the Mexican fin de siècle in which the obsession for progress affects the perceptions of bodies (Sarlo 28). As a dramatic change occurred in the representation of males at the end of the nineteenth century in Latin America, we are going to decode the text of male bodies to track the contradictions of Mexican modernity.

In the visual aspect of *modernismo*, the enjoyment of looking at male bodies—as bodies—is remarkable. The objectified male body means nothing less than the emergence of the male as an artistic object on a cultural horizon where religious, civic, and ethnographic views have constrained such representation. Rather than using the body to illustrate any doctrine or knowledge, *modernista* representation conveys the enjoyment of looking at the body as a sensory event. Consequently, there is no lack of sense, but rather a pretended lack of content—the absence of what in his *Critique of Judgement*, Kant defines as interest, when discussing dependent versus free beauty. In short, the reception of the nude male body states the *sense* of senses: the sensuality. The male body acquires this *sense* through what the act of looking at it implies.

Nudism refers to an enjoyment of the body, according to the Kantian principle of noninterested beauty, a principle we find in romanticism, Pre-Raphaelitism, symbolism, Parnassianism, decadentism, and all artistic movements that have been considered modern. Nevertheless, this detachment from moral, cognitive, and ideological dependency, does not lead to non-sense; rather, it points out the *sense*—or meaning and coherence—of the sensible. Through resistance to interest, the nude male body represents beauty in the manner of sensible intuition, which is equivalent to sensuality. Thus, pieces that claim to be perfect and beautiful do not still provide the body with intentionality.

Students from the Academia de San Carlos have worked hard to reproduce the Greek and Latin patterns of representation of bodies since the eighteen century (Velázquez 23). The Academia dictated the rules governing artistic representations of the body; it promoted a model originating in a long-ago legendary moment when the prototype was produced. Nudism thus connotes the mythical golden age, which furnishes the modern recreational space of the bourgeoisie. The sculptures of the Academia represent perfection. They serve as a lesson for students of sculpture and show what the human body should be: the "Doriphoros," reproduction of a sculpture by Policteto from Argos (ca. the fifth century BC), made by students of San Carlos ca. 1880 bears this inscription: "[I]n this piece the author defines the ideal proportions of human body." That belated neoclassical will, imagined in the eternal zone of pure aesthetics, appears in the context of modernization; it implements good taste, and it is free from content, or at least from the content that would contaminate Kantian immanence.

Such a classical immanence, that can refer to the origins of Western art appreciation, would be misunderstood, if we just considered it a belated coming to the history of art, the late arrival at the banquet of civilization, as Alfonso Reyes conceived Latin American modernity (Reyes 1978). In the patio of the Academia de San Carlos, we can appreciate that male representation actually entails or requires a patient task of imitation that westernizes the city and furnishes it with a modern taste. How does classical reiteration fulfill the meaning of modernity? In which moment does the classical become modern? When the iconography of the classics is nothing but a means of civilizing the colonized city, modernity emerges as a project of westernizing colonial taste and thus correcting it. The replica reflects a visual colonization. State sponsorship of this replica evidences the urge for or intention of civilizing the peripheral culture; that is the way the new republics must conform to the demands of capitalism. The representation of masculine body is a part of this colonization by the Western taste. Male representation is a matter of beauty, the distinctive expression that plays a key role in building modernity. In this sense, when talking about the male body and modernity, we refer to the artifact value of the body in the context of the lifestyle in a city that needs modernity. Since the founding of Real Academia de las Artes de San Carlos (1783), the urge for accelerating civilization has resulted in the import of nude male sculptures. Since then, they have been here; they function in the circulation of signs that makes the city; they are present in the dynamics of sights; and they participate in the flux of gazes. Looking at male bodies makes modernity possible.

From the beginning, these statues were intended to be didactic. They brought ideal beauty, perfect anatomy, and the model from which every human image should be produced. From the eighteenth century to the beginning of the twentieth, the Academia dictated the human image with models imported form European museums. Perfection came from Europe. This imaginary ruled on the stage of colonialism. But the consumption of these naked representations was restricted to the elite and was removed from national cultural trends. In 1890, José Juan Tablada summarizes this detachment of the art of the academy (or westernized art), as follows: " '[A]rte de aplicación' superpuesto y mal cosido a nuestro medio moral y social, arte que pocos practican, del que muchos fingen gustar y que la masa ignora y no comprende" (cit. in Moyssén 84) [Art of "appliqué" imposed and missewn on our moral and social environment, an art practiced by the few, which many pretend to enjoy, and which the masses ignore and misunderstand].

Tablada points out the contrast between elitist and what he considers national art. It consists of an ambiguity between a festive, relaxed, daily-life culture and melancholic expressions in the popular visual arts and songs. Regardless of this distance that Tablada observes, naked male sculptures arrived as part of modernity, and the national population experienced an eruption of European taste. Are these sculptures just didactic? If they are representations of what the human being should be, how close are the Mexican male bodies to the perfection of the Greek sculptures? The nude European male body is the sanctioned proposal of beauty, officially erected.

Regarding male bodies as objects that achieve the status of beauty is not as simple as it seems at first glance. It brings into consideration issues of gender roles and ethnicity. On the one hand, the male body becomes an object of admiration, if not of desire, in a society in which a man should be the subject who looks at the female body, who is considered the embodiment of beauty, according to hegemonic patriarchy. This twist in the role of who must look at whom, makes it necessary to elaborate a critique that uses the concept of beauty and sensuality to mediate between the gaze, determined as a gender role, and the presence of male body representations in public spaces. In the painting "Ex voto" (1910) by Ángel Zárraga, a woman prays on her knees in front of Saint Sebastian who poses seminaked in a sensual posture. The object of veneration is a male body. One of the best-known poems by the modernist writer Luis G. Urbina "El baño del centauro" depicts a pleasing scene of a naked man in the river being desired by an Indian woman (137).[3]

What are the meanings that this gaze on the male body convey? First of all, the appearance of sensuality conveys the meaning of enjoyment. If our aim is to find the meaning or sense of sensuality, we are not undertaking our analysis in the enchantment of hedonism but in its instrumentation. Its representation is an act and, in a very etymological sense, a politics: sensuality has a way of being in the web of discourses that form the modern polis. The naked male body comes to be a part of the lettered city as the pictorial parallel of the discursive construction of modernity. This civilizatory (politizating) way of occupying the public space norms or encodes the nude representation, makes sense of it, or puts its representation into a system of meanings, into a semantic field. What is the place of the male body in this signification? When we see the body, we read it. We have to discern and to select those cases that make sense regarding the understanding of the male body as articulated in Mexican modernity. This understanding places modernity in the field of images. It is a process of imaging; modern civilization is constituted as a performance: form persuading. We cannot but reprise the Lacanian conceptualization of the imaginary in which the self confronts the image. We have to elaborate this relationship in the field of historical subjectivity: the cultural self looks at the image that arose to make modernization visible. However, this historical subjectivity contains the normativity of bodily representations as if it were ahistorical.

According to Jesús Martín Barbero, Latin America experienced "una modernización cuya racionalidad, al presentarse como incompatible con su razón histórica, legitimó la voracidad del capital y la implantación de una economía que tornó irracional toda diferencia que no fuera recuperable por la lógica instrumental del mal llamado *desarrollo*" (Martín-Barbero 9) [a modernization whose rationality, while presenting itself as incompatible with historical reason, legitimated capitalism's voracity and the imposition of an economy that cast as irrational any difference that is not profitable in the instrumental logic of the ill-named development]. If modernity deals with differences in terms of instrumentalism for development, according to Martín-Barbero, masculine gender in the modern-colonial context is subject to the regulations of cultural requirements in modern capitalism. Masculinity is relocated and educated. The traditional-local is incorporated as part of modern-colonial dialogues if it is not extinguished for being a threat to "progress." Although it can be argued that Kantian principles of beauty, rather than the laws of consumption, provide intrinsic value to the representation of men, the uses of artistic artifacts determine their meaning.

Despite this norm of reception allowing the visibility of the masculine body in Mexico, sensuality, not masculinity, provides the content of the male body in *modernista* art. Nude male representation comes to the production-reception dialogue informed with sensualist aesthetics rather than with masculinity. This distinction is central to understanding that *modernista* sensuality is not referred to in terms of sexual desire and that we cannot flatly state that any kind of eroticism is explicitly depicted, although eroticism is constantly implied. Sensuality is constrained to a paradox consisting of an implicit eroticism and an explicit cult of form. This contradiction is made possible through a duplicity of codes: on the one hand, the piece of art is emptied of meaning, its symbolic reminiscence is accidental, ahistorical, fragmented, and the form—the sensitive objectification of the work—is targeted as the principle that validates the art piece; on the other hand, its uses do imply a content in terms of symbolic capital. Viewed sociologically, aestheticism takes shape within a socioeconomy of taste (Bourdieu 1984, 11). In the *modernismo* context, naked male representations would be more than a mere decorative artifact, a depositary of a value that structures the culture of reception. In this culture of reception we find a codification of the male body as a means of modernist education. The *modernista* sensuality modernizes male body, and this modernization consists of resignifying the pleasure of Greek nudist representation.

Somatic Modernity

If *modernista aesthetics* is considered ahistorical, exogenous, colonizing and uninterested (in Kantian terms), its practice does not constitute a field of meaning, but rather a field of disputed meanings. Addressing the intrinsic aspect of images is not the main criterion for interpreting the visual production of the Porfiriato; instead, we have to find in the juxtaposition of the modern and the national that composite, the term "the modern nation," the contradiction that confirms its historicity. The statues of the heroes on

Paseo de la Reforma and the nude sculptures of the Academia de San Carlos form the two main paths of male representations. However, the production of images of men is profuse as are the avenues of production and reception: the creation of a public, or the official pedagogy of the nation, is not the only modernizing project. The private art of the elite, the middle-class consumption of anonymous pieces, rustic religious objects, popular journalism, and cult magazines, all inform us of a perplexing web of visual communication, a diversity of iconographies and uses of images. It is not our goal to offer an exhaustive analysis of this complex field of meaning, but to discuss the valorizations of male images in the context of modernization.

Homi Bhabha offers a notion of the modern state that helps us reconsider the formation of Mexican modernity in terms of overlapping and of continuous metonymy in the writing of the nation, which needs "to inscribe the ambivalent and chiasmic intersections of time and place that constitute the problematic 'modern' experience of the western nation" (293).[4] Representations that intersect, at some conflictive point, significant contamination that perturbs the intended sense of the artistic work, and the visual and the written signs of modernity seem to postpone very often the project of westernization. Julio Ramos observes that the *modernista* chronicle concentrates on the contradictions of modernization, revealing precisely a conflicted dissemination of meaning (Julio Ramos 113).

In the literature of the period, it is important to underscore the intervention of naturalism in the *modernista* text when describing sensuality as a destructive experience. In the novella *Pascual Aguilera* by Amado Nervo (1892), we find the characterization of the male body dependent on the emergent and unavoidable imperative of sensuality. Pascual Aguilera lives with his stepmother after the death of his father. In elementary school he was a troublemaker and sexually precocious, which prevented him from completing his basic education. Pascual refused to be educated. Punishment and reprimand were useless in controlling his sexual compulsivity. Although sensuality is related to modern civilization, as Robert M. Irwin suggests in his comments on Luis G. Urbina's chronicles (Irwin 2003, 61), in Nervo's narrations it is not a result of education. Pascual's characterization is based on the assumption that there is an uncultivable sexual nature in the male body. This naturalist view states that there is an essentialist, precivilizing norm that emerges from the body. While most of *modernista* and naturalist narratives are located in artificial scenes of the urban decadence—apparent in works of Manuel Gutiérrez Nájera, Federico Gamboa, and Tomás Pérez de Cuéllar—*Pascual Aguilera*'s space depicts a rural, traditional, quasifeudal society. It cannot not be considered a modern space; it is rather a dimension negated by modernity. Carlos Monsiváis, in his chronicle about Nervo's life, points out the contradiction between provincial Catholicism and the audacious transgressions of Nervo's characters (Monsiváis 2002, 87). Concurring with the idea that modernity consists of a process of civilization that is the construction of the *civitas*, Monsiváis observes that Nervo seems to be a less modern writer in his rural fiction. Rather than a story of decadence, where the city and fin de siècle spiritual breakdown shape the character's fate, in *Pascual Aguilera* modernity comes from inside, as a natural correction of traditional repressive systems.

Aguilera's family owns the estate. This position allows him to seduce and sexually abuse practically all women serving the family. The exception is Rosario, who always rejects his harassment. Rosario and Santiago marry and Pascual's sexual requests for Rosario do not succeed. Then, on the wedding night, Pascual mistakes his stepmother (a religious woman who never had experienced an orgasm) for Rosario. Pascual rapes his stepmother and then dies of a brain hemorrhage. If the male's sexual appetite is not satisfied, madness and death are ineluctable. This naturalist fiction proposes that male sexuality is out of the control of social rules. The body's norm then transcends social morality.

In his novella *El Bachiller* (1895), Nervo presents a conflict between religious norm and sexuality. Felipe, a teenager, has decided to be a priest, but in his visit to his uncle's farm, where he is convalescing from rheumatic pain, Asunción, the woman who took care of him, tries to convince him with erotic contact to renounce his vocation. In a dramatic ending, Felipe commits suicide while Asunción is touching him erotically. Asunción blames Felipe for deserting "una vida donde sus energías pueden significar mucho en bien de sus semejantes" (198) [a life where his energy could mean a lot for his fellows' welfare]. A neoplatonic law of attraction renders, in Asunción's words, an argument against the church's rejection of eroticism. A philosophic reflection on the body's attraction suggests that Nervo's liberal agenda, as a natural disposition opposed to feudal Catholic rules, introduces a civilizing position against the Spanish colonial order. In Nervo's discourse we can recognize the sensual theology that characterized some reflections of Spanish fin de siècle writers–Alas Clarín, Unamuno, and Pío Baroja. Nervo's enlightenment inserts liberal sensuality at the pivotal moment when, through fatal explosion, the body responds to the countererotic law. If for Nervo modernization is not a question of education, but of the natural requirements of the body, modernity consists of a discourse of the body that is a somatic symbolic system.[5] According to this view, civilization is based on the discovery of the body, the attention to bodily signs, and the hermeneutics of symptoms. This "discovery" is nothing but the articulation of the discourse of the body. In *Pascual Aguilera*, the doctor's explanation of Aguilera's death offers an instance of this bodily discourse: "una hemorragia cerebral con inundación ventricular, ocasionada por una intensa conmoción fisiológica debida a histeria mental" (184) [a cerebral hemorrhage with a ventricular flow originated in an intense physiological commotion due to mental hysteria]. The body is explained, categorized, and pathologized in medical terms. Fin de siècle is the historical period when body becomes an object of scientific discipline, a text woven with the language of symptoms, as Foucault observes (25–47).

Both naked bodies from the Academia and explosive bodies in the narrations by Amado Nervo are expressions of somatic modernity. In the sculptures of the Academia de San Carlos, the naked body symbolizes modernization by means of European aesthetics. In Nervo's novellas, modernization is interpreted as an inner structure inscribed in the body's rejection of the traditional norms that control it. Internalized rejection is a term that describes the representation of the mestizo. Race and desire are intertwined in most literary works of Mexican *modernismo* and naturalism. In texts like "Mi Inglés" by Manuel Gutiérrez Nájera, "Si Fueras Inglés" by Amado Nervo and the intriguing novella by Federico Gamboa, *La Excursionista*, we can trace this intrinsic rejection.

In Gutiérrez Nájera's "Mi inglés" a Mexican man visits the mansion of a British gentleman. They walk along the galleries and gardens, where we can recognize all the paraphernalia of the *modernista* imagination: the art nouveau architecture, Pre-Raphaelite painting, as well as sculpture and furniture with mythological themes from all around the world. The accumulation of beautiful objects arranged by the logic of adornment—beyond any content that provides coherence to this diversity of forms—introduces meaning that can be appreciated as excess, providing grandeur to the character, whose value is found in his collection. This story is organized, then, from the viewpoint of a narrator whose discourse constructs the other's magnificence. That other possesses the valuable goods: power, taste, knowledge, and the object of desire—not only the collection of art pieces, but also a beautiful woman who never is disclosed to the narrator's gaze. The fact that taste consists of an accumulation of exquisite objects reflects the quantitative sense of *modernista* aestheticism. If the collection of various objects is the value to be achieved, being a British gentleman would be an attainable goal, after all. As Graciela Montaldo observes, in *modernismo* beauty is accessible in the market (13). We can extend this accessibility that the British gentleman represents to the Mexican visitor, and propose that the colonialist aspect of *modernismo* consists of making Western values a benefit that European imperial markets make available to non-European countries.

Modernity consists of a process of dissemination of forms as commodities, and the divulgence of ideas through the channels and webs that free-trade imperialism has established. It is an accelerated and seemingly dispersed and fragmented movement of materials, concepts, and life styles. It is, in sum, a zone of contacts and influences (Montaldo 15). This is not, according to Montaldo, a simple mimesis, but rather the conversion of mimesis into the artificial and the unnatural, closer to the performance of imitation rather than the imitation per se. As we observed in the sculptures of the Academia, and in general the *modernista* art, the consumption of European products and icons leads to the fetishism of European fashion as a social rule (Macías 227). Hence, being modern means being dressed like the imperial other, that is, being the receptor of the imperial forms. Artificiality is a condition that problematizes the cultural self-display that only values exogenous letters, products, icons, signs—in short a masquerade that pursues pure appearance beyond the self. The artificial compulsivity invents the performance of colonization. If there is a politics of the artificial, it is the diffusion of an integrated universe of fragments from the world whose possession provides the colonized conscience with the experience of civilization. The forms that we can see in Nájeras' "Mi inglés" are not precisely European forms but the forms that the European imperialism acquires through the diffusion of the liberal market. When the British gentleman appears as a cosmopolitan subject, he embodies the model of the Western masculinity. The narrator's gaze is in the presence of an unattained masculine norm. The positions of the British gentleman and the Mexican spectator are asymmetric. Their interaction is characterized by the admiration of the latter for the abundance of the former. The British gentleman is signified by all the objects in his collection, while the Mexican visitor's role in this oneiric story is to be absorbed in the desire for the artificial. We can establish that this desiring gaze evidences the construction of the modern-colonized masculinity, which is produced not just by imitation but also by self-denial, reducing this subjectivity to gazing at the magnificence of the imperial other. Instead of the Western masculine model proposed by Michael Kimmel, which consists of the achievement of success through the sacrifice and the stoicism that characterize Western males (50–51), the Mexican man is oriented toward reception of the performance of the Western male's image; therefore, simulation makes a significant difference between the conqueror and the conquered male.

A myriad of *modernista* chronicles portrays the author's amazement at what he has only heard about Paris, as in the case of Gutiérrez Nájera's, who has never traveled to Europe, but relies on second-hand details about Parisian life. Newspapers and magazines during the Porfiriato updated readers about the art and theater schedules of this city. Male dress and cosmetics constructed fetishistic bodies. "Culetear la boquilla" by Amado Nervo is all about the sacrifices necessary for obtaining an elegant pipe; "Baile y cochino" by Pérez de Cuéllar entertains the reader with descriptions of dress and accessories, implying a code of colors and forms that emphasize the sensual reading of the body. Mexican men, according to Víctor Macías, were sophisticated and very involved in the construction of the appearance (233); these observations describe modernity in Mexico as a delightful suggestivity of senses.

Dressing to mislead, to seduce, to confuse; dressing to obtain the other's appearance; dressing to climb the social ladder (when being like the European is a mark of prestige): such are the constant motifs in the literature of the naturalism and *modernismo* decades. In Amado Nervo's "Si fueras inglés" Mariquita, a girl who is alienated by reading European novels, rejects marriage with her boyfriend Juan because he is not a British gentleman, only a Mexican man. Juan then disappears. After a time, a British gentleman moves to town and meets Mariquita at a party. The girl fulfills her desire without knowing that her dream British gentleman is in fact her Mexican ex-boyfriend pretending to be British. In another short story by Nervo, "Aventura de carnaval," a young man complains of not finding love. His cousin, Carlos, who is described as an effeminate man, challenges him and bets that he will fall in love that night. In fact, the skeptical cousin does fall in love with a girl whose eyes captivate him until he finally discovers that he has actually succumbed to Carlos's transvestite seduction, a joke played at the young man's expense.

One of the stories that may be read as emblematic of Porfirian transvestism is the novella by Federico Gamboa "La Excursionista." A Texan bandit travels to Mexico dressed as a woman. Miss Eva arrives in Mexico City and rents an apartment far from the American tourists that "she" traveled with on the same train from El Paso, Texas. Fernando, a *lagartijo* (a type of well-dressed male who spent time in the streets of Mexico City harassing high-class ladies), insists on dating Miss Eva without success, despite several visits and gifts. In the last pages of the story, Miss Eva accepts his invitation to a private room in an elegant restaurant. At an (in)opportune moment, Fernando tries to kiss her, but Miss Eva interrupts his kiss to reveal "her" masculine identity. Fernando feels so ashamed that he never allows himself to be seen in public again.

The relationship between the foreigners and the nationals is determined by the semiotics of dress. European and American identities are performed through the artificiality of appearance. For Angel Rama, one aspect of democratization in the *modernista* era is access to utilitarian goods (19–20). Rama associates a utilitarian attitude with hedonism, with the pleasure without the substance that the accumulation of objects means, to the enjoyment of the possession of the forms—the enjoyment of the gestures—that can make being European equivalent to being Mexican. Rather than demonstrating or implying that this hedonism is an emptiness or lack of substance, this proliferation of objects initiates a meaningful and complex process of colonization that can be understood as desire in the capitalist system that Deleuze and Guattari propose in their book *Anti-Oedipus*. Desire establishes not only value, but also the power relationship (Deleuze and Guattari 60). Then modernity in Mexico can be interpreted in terms of excess in desiring the exogenous, and hence becoming a body of pleasure and consumption. The modern male body is then a deployment of hedonism that is ciphered in terms of desire: power produced at the level of seduction as a form of conquest by the liberalist economy.

The subject of transvestism appears in a large number of works during the Porfiriato. Robert M. Irwin and Carlos Monsiváis show how the famous scandal of The 41, a ball where 20 men were discovered dressed as women, produced a series of representations (José Guadalupe Posada's drawings, the novel *Los 41: Novela Crítica Social* by Eduardo A. Castrejón, and several newspaper articles) in which, effeminacy is related to the European influence on Mexico City's upper class. In all the expressions regarding this issue, the artificiality of dress and the sensuality of masculine bodies are an effect of the fin de siècle modernity. According to Buffington, transvestism in Mexico has been used to disempower political enemies. In the case of the 41, as well as in the examples of political caricature analyzed by Buffington, the devaluation of the body depends on dress (197–200). This reading of the body's appearance opens further discussion of the body as signified by only gestures, performance and drag. This is so even for the naked bodies of the Academia and the naturalness attempted in narrations like "Pascual Aguilera," where a completely natural characterization of the male body can be interpreted in terms of a performative politics; that is, using the naked body for performing the idea of normative beauty (in the sculpture cases) makes bodies decorative artifacts for a society that gestures modernity. On the other hand, using the body of the hypersexualized male, as in the Pascual Aguilera case, offers the argument that modernity can liberate natural instincts such as male sexuality.

Modernizing Natives

The irruption of the body into discourses is thus a modernizing intervention. The male body plays a central role in this intervention when the meaningless (uninterested) pretension of European art becomes a meaningful entanglement of the bodies that represent the nation (the heroes, the Indians, the mestizos). The national bodies in the nineteenth century had included the sacred image of the fathers of the nation after independence—limited to the iconography of official discourse—and the *costumbrista* depiction of Mexican types, which continues the ethnographic categorization in the *castas* paintings from the colonial period into the nineteenth century.[6] This idealization of the national body constitutes the antecedents in which the denationalizing *modernista* body emerges. The value of aestheticism, universal and individualistic, has to overcome the nationalist rhetoric, replacing it as artistic content; nevertheless, the representation-invention of the national body is not expelled from the iconographic catalogue of the period dominated by the *modernista* aesthetics. The narrative of the nation's folk, the collective type that embodies the nation, in the sense of the people in Herder's and de Vico's works, becomes the narrative of the sensualized indigenous. In the *costumbrista* style, scenes of a dramatized daily life lead us to focus on ethnic features that turn our gaze to their emblems, dresses, or actions.

Undoubtedly, *modernismo* introduces a sensual codification to this *costumbrista* iconography as a means of depicting racial specificities. Nevertheless, sensualization of national types is already observable in works by the most important *costumbrista* painter, José Agustín Arrieta, who in his "Pulquerías" and "Requiebros" provides the mestizo with sexual connotation, focusing on the body and the gestures rather than on dress and symbols. Proposing iconographies that overcome the purely European content, as seen in the public sculptures of the Porfiriato, popular drawings such as Manilla's and José Guadalupe Posada's focus on representations of mestizos. With violent depiction that coincides with the criminal-essentialist discourse of the period (Irwin et al. 4; Piccato 251–266), mestizo and Indian characters represent the opposite end of the civilizatory image proposed by the aestheticism of the academic art. The decadence of religiosity in the post-Reform society is interpreted as decadence in the naturalist literature, as well as in works about criminal issues and in prints by popular illustrators. Nervo's Pascual Aguilera and his sexual incontinence is not the only excessive depiction of the male body's explosive subordination to fleshly appetites. Criminal stories and pictures in popular pamphlets provide a version of the popular that overcomes the schematization or misunderstanding of the mestizo and the Indian in costumbrista art. Modernismo is not only a Latin American interpretation of European fin de siècle art, but also a subjectification of the national body, in contrast with romantic and costumbrista interpretations consisting of external and emblematic objectification.

In the same way that Judith Butler observes that abjection in the social discourses incorporates rejected bodies into the symbolic system by making them a public issue by means of reiteration (1993, 8), the depiction of the criminal mestizo in the popular publications opens the way for reflection on the subjectivity of the mestizo. With the construction of national identity projected by romanticism, the Indian body was employed as the allegorical body of the nation. But it was a body corrected and idealized; Indian bodies were seminaked and anatomically shaped under the normative academic body. This idealized and Eurocentric ethnography, called Indianismo, proposes European aesthetics, proportions, and even facial features as a means of beautifying the primitive (uncultivated) Indian body. It means that the Indian, being one of the main national icons since independence, is produced according to the norms of European aesthetics, providing nationalism with a colonized interpretation of the self.

There are two forms of Indian representation in romantic art: the one where the Indian is an element of the landscape, or is located in the margin of the scene; and the one where the Indian is an idealized hero. Both gestures normalize the Indian to the European eyes. The romantic Indian is not a subject itself but merely a schematic conceptualization of the unknown as recourse of its appropriation. The *other*, defined as unknown reminds us of Levinas' fatalistic definition of the other as the unrevealed (52). The problem of the national body's image is itself the problem of colonialism. The pictorial language conforms to the ethnographic gaze of the European subject. It means that aesthetic colonialism practiced in the Academia retains the misunderstanding that constructs the native other. In the end, however, *modernista* art achieves an interpretation of the national mestizo and Indian body, characterizing them with sensual expressiveness. With the construction of criminal popular images, such as "el Tigre de Santa Julia" or Goyo Cárdenas—hypersexualized and cruel characters of popular mythology—the mestizo and the Indian acquire, with their excess of sensuality, a perturbing image that shows the contradictions of the modernity. In the extremism we find in the prints by Posada, Manilla, and Ruelas, we can observe the confluence of European decadentism and the representations of non-European nationals as subjects inclined to excess. As the preurbanization consolidating structures of the church and the hacienda abandon the national subjects, urbanization produces decadence. The horror of modern times has in Posada an apocalyptic feature. Extraordinary phenomena, diseases and all kinds of criminal events, are interrelated to reinforce the guilt for breaking the traditional premodern order. In their fiction, Federico Gamboa and Pérez de Cuéllar seem to agree with this view, as they extract from the naturalist aesthetics a national criminal constructed in the body of the mestizo. Vices are associated with the migration from the countryside to the city; prostitution is the destiny of women who have broken the patriarchal rule; transvestism consists of the shame of losing virility among the urban middle and upper classes.

Modernization not only constructs a threat to the ancient régime but also provides the mestizo and Indian with a sensual body. In the second period of pictorial *modernismo*, works by Saturnino Herrán explore the physiognomy and gesture of the Indian as a body of enjoyment. In 1917, the cover of the magazine *Pegaso* presented his picture "El guerrero" [the warrior]. It is a drawing made with charcoal on paper that, according to Fausto Ramírez, conjugates a neomannerist taste with an erotic symbolism readable in the arrow and the powerful anatomy presented with difficult postures. Anatomy and intentionality describe sensuality in Herrán's works. The warrior pose opens the possibility of a sensual meaning—that is, a meaning that comes from the body—extracting from it a taste for enjoying the Indian body as an object of desire. The protagonist looks at the target of his attack, while the spectator is directed to focus on his anatomical display; the gesture of being an object of the spectator's gaze is inscribed in the picture as the signifying dynamics.

With respect to Herrán's works, Manuel Toussaint stated, "Herrán ha logrado no sólo el arte más mexicano que ha habido, puesto que en él viven en integridad todas las inquietudes y fuerzas latentes, sino marcar el derrotero que ha de seguir el *mexicanismo* en el arte cuando quiera ser algo más que pasatiempo decorativo" (13) [Herrán has achieved not only the most Mexican art ever, because his work integrates all latent forces and anxieties, but has also traced the way of Mexicanismo in art, when it is intended as more than a mere decorative pastime]. These comments by Toussaint present Herrán as a nondecorative nationalist painter. To prefigure a national art, just at the time when revolution is in process, conveys a criticism of the Díaz regime and the aesthetics of *modernismo* as colonized, dependent art. The national question arose again and the body came to be a national signifier. But Herrán is still *modernista*, and perhaps the most mature of *modernista* painters. What makes him a nationalistic part of *modernismo* is the sensualization of the nation through male bodies. With Herrán national sensuality starts the art of the revolution.

In his speech at Herrán's funeral, "Oración fúnebre" [funeral prayer] López Velarde stated, "Su sensualidad . . . fundamenta su obra . . . Ya no habrá virilidad; poco importa, pues resta el vino de

Mosela que embotellamos en la hermosa edad parabólica" (261) [his sensuality supports his works . . . There will no longer be virility; that is not important, as the Mosela wine that we bottled in the beautiful parabolic age remains]. The alchemy of physical perception that structures the Indian bodies in Herrán's paintings shows that soul is distant from human experience while sensuality is the experience of life itself. The mention of virility calls attention to something that is lost but nevertheless preserved, as the wine is. For Velarde, this sensual virility that is preserved by the representation defines Herrán's work. In this representative semiotics and in the male image that carries implications for the national and the colonial consciousness, we can find the keys to the inner movement of modern Mexico's imaginary history.

3

The Perturbing Dress: Transvestism in Visual Arts

This chapter describes how the representation of transvestite men interacts with Mexican culture and politics from the Porfirato to the last decades of the twentieth century. I will emphasize the relationship between transvestism and national identity from two perspectives: one, the exclusionary view that condemns effeminacy considering it an antinational mark, an ideological enemy, and a symptom of decadence; and the other, the recognition of the transvestite as an instrument of criticism of social prejudices and as a exploder which destabilizes identities. The discussion of visual representations of transvestites makes us recognize the Mexican gender system from the viewpoint of its most deconstructive character. As in the sensualization of the male body through nudism we studied in chapter 2, in the representation of the dressed male with nonvirile clothing, we can observe that the limits of the national are readable in the representation of men.

The Politics of Transvestism

If sensuality is perceived as the configuration of the bodily experience as an external—but not insignificant—sign, transvestism expresses the culmination of the visual sensuality. Transvestism cannot be interpreted by merely examining the appearance; it is by itself a plastic art event in which the body is nothing but its exteriority. Thus, it is imprecise to call transvestism a sexuality; it is rather a kind of eroticism consummated within an exterior's limits. Transvestism has therefore become a synonym for performance as well as gender, as Marjorie Garber suggests (143). The representation of the transvestite in Mexican art from the Porfiriato through contemporary times is an indicator of the evolution of the history of gender issues during the twentieth century in Mexico. As we have already mentioned, political cartoons in newspapers since the nineteenth century have represented transvestites as political enemies in a derogatory and enfeebling manner, implying that to womanize an individual is crippling or emasculating (Buffington 199). Posada's cartoons of "Los Cuarenta y uno" develop the main traces of homophobic fear: men stay at home to perform domestic tasks; they appear in the middle of the street and are subjected to public scorn while they sweep or walk to the train that will take them to their mandated exile in Yucatan; some of these drawings depict the ball that took place in a bourgeois house on the street Calle de la Paz in November of 1901 (see figure 3.1). On the one hand, Posada condemns transvestites to the private sector and emphasizes that a man should not wear women's dresses; on the other hand, transvestism is interpreted as a political critique of the ruling Porfirato's bourgeoisie class. In this sense, Posada's etchings function as a means of private exhibition in which those who congregate around the transvestite in the "cuarenta y uno" cartoons are depicted as belonging to the lower class. The *lagartijos* and the transvestites are symbolically defeated because of this "outing" from their enclosed circle into the public sphere. In the iconographic universe of Posada, these masculine characters have been identified as *lagartijos*, whose frock coats and long twisted mustaches are part of the outfit of a French-influenced dominant class of the Porfiriato. Transvestites, then, had to be considered *lagartijos* in women's dresses. That is, rather than being opposites, *lagartijos* and transvestites are two facets of the same characterization.

In 1901, the general public witnessed the emergence of a line of exclusion in the press, similar to that of the man who was born with three legs, the women who tortured children, and the man who killed his wife: that morbid imagination we can find in the graphics by Manilla, Ruelas, and Posada, the disastrous plebeian

Corrido "LOS 41"

Figure 3.1 José Guadalupe Posada *Corrido "los 41"* [*Balad "the 41"*]. Courtesy of Benson Latin American Collection, The University of Texas at Austin.

competence that academic artist disdained, according to Jean Charlot (5). Whether he is perceived as criminal or simply a misguided product of nature, the transvestite is portrayed in the space of quotidian images as a social disease. He is the most conspicuous piece of evidence suggesting the decadence of the Porfirian regime. The addressees of these etchings are the same who utilize *corridos* as a means of information and expression. Therefore, the transvestite body is inscribed in the popular imagination in the list of scandals and apocalyptic events that punish the sins of modernity: earthquakes, floods, and the iniquitous actions of transvestites that nurtured popular literature and journalism. However, the transvestism is neither an action nor an event; it is an unfolding of the derogation of the naturalness of gender; it is a nauseous presence that blows up the strings of abjection. Kristeva has stated that abjection is an irrational compulsion, a corporeal reaction to a transgression of the symbolic system (2–3). The spontaneous rejection of the policeman who came to the ball to stop the private party at Calle de la Paz shows a collapse between signs (the cross-dressed men) and the body (his distressed stomach) (cit. in Irwin, McCaughan, and Nasser 35). The consequence of wearing women's dresses consists of designifying the masculine-feminine gender difference, that is, reducing gender to a question of costumes.

The transvestite is then a materialization of abjection; he makes possible the emergence of exclusion by constructing fences against the derogation of measures and distinctions. The etchings of Posada serve to point out this abjection. They allude to the rejection of the strange body, and for that, as Monsiváis observes, its existence has to be recognized first (1998:2, 18). Combined with rejection, abjection creates a field of meaning that goes beyond acceptable representations. This paradox reveals that Posada's works, which are crossed by the presence of the rejected, bear within themselves the resistance to their own intended rejection. There is not abjection that can escape the realm of signification.

Since the publication of French artist Jean Charlot's articles on Posada and Manilla in 1926 in the magazine *Forma*, these artists have been considered the direct predecessors of revolutionary art. The representation of transvestism takes place on the stage of the nation. Porfirian popular iconography attains official status through the interpretations of Charlot and Diego Rivera. The depiction of the transvestite as a body that should be rejected is a persistent element in staging of male imagery: it is a force that constrains and outlines masculinity.

It is not accurate to attribute to Posada and Manilla the kernel of Mexican postrevolutionary iconography. Although the influence of these popular engravers can be confirmed in the works of Diego Rivera and Antonio Ruiz el Corcito, or even Abel Quezada's cartoons, we cannot ignore the fact that the sensuality of Saturnino Herrán and Roberto Montenegro has influenced Manuel Rodríguez Lozano, Tebo, and Abraham Álgel. In addition, we also can observe that the *pathos* of Francisco Goitia is echoed in the torments of José Clemente Orozco, Frida Khalo, and David Alfaro Siqueiros. *The revolution did not cause any rupture in art history. Most of the artists that produced their works during and shortly after the 1920s were educated in the Porfirian regime academy, when the government had already been fostering nationalist representations.* Effeminacy and transvestism reiterated in modern Mexican art parallel official representations of the nation. As in works of Posada and other political caricaturists of the Porfiriato, in works by Rivera and Antonio Ruiz, effeminacy and transvestism are used for derogating political enemies: the counterrevolutionary and antinational are shown cross-dressed in order to be ridiculed. Thus, the dispute over national character results in a political interpretation of clothing.

Apart from the fear of transvestism dismounting the heterosexual order, there is also the fear of the transvestite becoming desirable. We can infer from these fears the reason for compulsive repudiation, disgust, nausea, and anxiety depicted in the representations of the transvestite. The scorn for the transvestite promoted by revolutionary culture does more than devaluate his image; it codifies him as the fearful subject, promoting him as a symbolic force integrated into the semiotic dynamics of the visual arena. While Diego Rivera's murals illustrate the national representation of virility, the works of Abraham Ángel, Agustín Lazo, Tebo, Ángel Zárraga, Manuel Rodríguez Lozano, and Roberto Montenegro smoothen the masculine body by depicting man's sexual objectification and seductive effeminacy. Roberto Montenegro's *Mateo*, portrays a muscular man with African features holding a basketful of fish while he turns his torso with pronounced mannerisms. The colorful background is a field covered with tropical foliage, and the racialized body and his posture are reminiscent of the overly sensual Indian we observed in Saturnino Herrán's works, but now in a clearly effeminate mulatto role. Whereas in Herrán, many of the dancing character's poses create a deployment without eye contact with the spectator, in Montenegro, the character focuses his intense attention on the one who stands toward the canvas. Montenegro represents the objectification of the viewers; Herrán assigns them the active role in the desiring relationship.

The desiring gaze has been cultivated by the group related to the cultural magazines *Falange, Cultura*, and *Los Contemporáneos*, and the theater company *Ulises* in the 1920s and 1930s. What Rudi C. Bleys calls "the homosexual gaze" when talking about Rodríguez Lozano's paintings (101), becomes an iconographic motif that we can also find in portrayals of men by Adolfo Best Maugard, Abraham Ángel, Tebo, Roberto Montenegro, Agustín Lazo, and Emilio Baz Viaud. How can a gaze be the central factor of effeminacy? In his chronicle "Ojos que da pánico soñar" [Eyes that cause panic when dreamed], José Joaquín Blanco offers a series of adjectives that describe this gaze: "sesgadas, fijas, lujuriosas, sentimentales, socarronas, rehuyentes, ansiosas, rebeldes, serviles, irónicas" (1981, 83) [slanted, fixed, lecherous, sentimental, sarcastic, evasive, anxious, rebellious, servile, and ironic]. A mixture of defensiveness, desire, and submissiveness is articulated in this reading of the homosexual gaze. Rather than a mere feminine look, we can observe in this representation the traces of a complex relationship between the homosexual and the repulsion he has to face either by seducing, reacting with bitterness, or by subjecting himself to the society's scorn. Probably one of the most intensive gazes, undoubtedly the premonition of the early suicidal comes from the eyes of Abraham Ángel's self-portraits: all the torment produced by the rejection is coded in those eyes that condense the whole gamut of adjectives that Blanco has used.

There are, therefore, two possible paths when considering the representation of effeminate males: one that conveys the derogatory depiction of Posada's etchings of the "cuarenta y uno" scandal, and the other that is astonished by the complexity of the homosexual gaze. In fact, we can talk about a symbolic dispute that takes place in the field of men's effeminacy that reveals the destabilization of gender as it carries out and transcends into the destabilization of aesthetic norms. The various portrayals of Salvador Novo made by artists subscribing to both of the aforementioned symbolic ideologies probably constitute the most significant and problematic iconographic representations of the effeminate man in Mexican art.

In 1924, Manuel Rodríguez Lozano portrayed Novo with slanted eyes, rouged lips, manicured nails, and a sort of colorful robe or feminine dress, sitting inside an urban bus. In the background, looking through the window of the bus we can see the Central Post Office building located on the corner of Tacuba and San Juan de Letrán Avenue (now Eje Central) and the movements of a lively night in Mexico City. It seems to be Novo's outfit for cruising. The presence of the buses refers to Salvador Novo's preference for public bus drivers who, besides being his occasional sexual partners, invited Novo to publish in their Union newsletter. The composition shows the space of seduction, the posture of the effeminate seducer; that is, the configuration of a role (being the seducer); the encoding of a space (the street in movement, which is the mobile space for cruising, where gazes navigate among the desirable bodies), and a time (the night that belongs to the homosexual for seeking a partner). This portrayal articulates a body with its specific context as a sign of the modernity that implies a threat to gender norms.

The painting *Los paranoicos* by Antonio Ruiz el Corcito includes among other subjects a characterization of Novo. This piece depicts the group of *Los Contemporáneos* walking the street in a vigorous march, a sort of combative carnival. Misusing, diverting, deviating, corrupting, are some of the connotations of the word *perversion*. It is the antipode of the good gender sense. Bodies such as that of Novo develop a proactive convulsion. The painting portrays the panic that is created by this disruptive gang. Dandyism, extravagance, and transvestism, meet together to represent the catalogue of the feared bodies, that is, the feared dresses, which can be also interpreted as a feared modernity.

In the murals by Diego Rivera in the office building of the Secretaría de Educación Pública in Mexico City, we find the image of Salvador Novo represented in two panels. In the one entitled *Día de muertos* (1923) [The Day of the Dead], Novo peeps at the multitude from the left side. His eyebrows are plucked, and his eyes look obliquely toward the spectator as he dons a sarcastic smile. On the right side of the panel, we can see Rivera's face without makeup, implying the frankness and simplicity of his virility that contrasts with the complications of Novo's cosmetics. The confrontation of these faces with each other reiterates the dispute about the male body in the controversies on national culture that appeared in Mexico City's newspapers in 1925 and 1932. Male representations have been, since then, a question of national identity. Víctor Días Arciniegas and Guillermo Sheridan, among others, have studied meticulously the terms of these polemics, underscoring that the definition of revolutionary culture depends on a divergence between virility and effeminacy. For nationalist artists, effeminacy connotes falseness, weakness, foreign corruption or colonization, and a perverted position from which ambiguity makes the effeminate male a betrayer and a destructive subject.

In the panel *El que quiera comer que trabaje*, Rivera represents himself pushing Novo with his foot, while Novo, depicted with donkey ears kneels on his hands and knees. María Antonieta Rivas Mercado sweeps away among other things an issue of the *Revista Contemporáneos*. A peasant and a worker dominate the scene from the upper side; their rigid and arrogant attitude contrasts with Novo's humiliating posture. In the center of the panel, a woman with a rifle and cartridge belt leads the rest of the characters. She is a virilized woman; therefore, Rivera's representation of the revolutionary also transgresses heterosexual representations. The masculinized woman is a prominent character in the narratives of the revolution; Francisco Rojas González's novel *La negra Angustias* and Ismael Rodríguez's film *La cucaracha* have cross-dressed women who play a leading role. Virility is reiterated as the way the revolutionary state should appear, even when this means to "pervert" womanhood. Therefore, we can observe that both revolutionary modernity and the modernity accused of being antirevolutionary and effeminate consist of transgressing heterosexual models.

Responding to the gender-related political comment conveyed in Rivera's murals, Salvador Novo's satires incorporate the image of Diego Rivera, resulting in a deconstruction of virility. In "La diegada," Novo represents Diego Rivera as an impotent man: "Las furias asombra tamaño conjuro,/ que aquel cuya panza tomaron por frente/ no puede ante el muro lograr ponteduro/ con mano que empuña pincel deficiente" (14) [This conjure amazes furies:/ this one whose belly was confused as a forehead/ cannot succeed his erection at the wall/ with his hand that holds his deficient brush]. The monumental pamphlet of Rivera's murals is sterile to the eyes of Novo. At the two extremes of the virile-effeminate dispute, the accusations are similar. The virile artists blame the effeminacy that is associated with the practicing of empty, false, and superficial ornamental art. In the same way, Novo blames Rivera for being reiterative in his hyperbolic and simplistic aesthetic of political pamphlets.

As we observed in a previous work (Domínguez 126–129), Salvador Novo's satires are mostly dedicated to the deconstruction of the strategies of authentication of the virile male in revolutionary art. Heroes perform history with their clothing and gestures of the puppets (Novo 109). We find in the exterior construction of heroes, in their clothing, a statement that defines the transvestite's condition of virility. Novo rejects this strategy for stigmatization of effeminacy when he shows that masculinity, regardless of its representation as virile or effeminate, is a question of one's manner of dressing. Therefore, the pretended frankness and lack of cosmetics in Rivera's self-portrayal are, in fact, intended to be a strategic performance of virility. The absence of cosmetics can be interpreted as an absence of effeminacy rather than an affirmation of virility. In other words, this suggests that virility should be understood in terms of one's denial of the feminine. There is no virility without homophobic compulsion. If virility describes or allegorizes the nation, then homophobia outlines the nation.

Although a critique of machismo has been at the center of the reflection on the Mexican national identity since the 1930s, as we will be discussing in chapter 6, homophobic compulsion remains a criterion for distinguishing between the national (virile) and the antinational (effeminate) in public discourses of the postrevolutionary era. The cartoonist Abel Quezada, for instance, continued to produce representations of the transvestite until the 1970s in the same way as Rivera and Ruiz did. It confirms that the hegemonic discourse forged by the revolutionary elite imagining the nation in terms of virility. Nevertheless, Quezada's cartoons appear crossed by the seductive resistance of the transvestite. In the cartoon "Presagios de primavera" [Springtime Premonitions] published in the newspaper *El Excélsior* on March 4, 1971, Quezada focuses on alerting the public against the danger that transvestism poses: that it may erode virility and therefore the national culture. A cross-dressed character wears fashionable garments that unfold gender neutrality by blurring the difference between masculinity and femininity. In the next frame, the same character appears wearing hot pants. The character seems uncomfortable with this feminine garb and expresses disgust over it. However, gradually, this man is lured by the idea of wearing it: "no insistan. ¡No! ¡No! Ay . . . ¿En qué colores vienen?" [Do not insist. No! No! Oh . . . What colors are available?]. On the one hand, this cartoon conforms to the idea that effeminacy is a foreign (antinational) influence, and therefore the seduction of fashion must be rejected; on the other hand, this man is weak and cannot avoid being introduced to the prohibited fascination with color. The male is seduced by dresses; an unexpected attraction for cross-dressing is enough to erase his virility and the nation in one stroke.

Erasing gender marked by cross-dressing becomes a battlefield where the exteriors of the masculine and the feminine are easily exchangeable. In "La guerra de los sexos" (*El Excélsior* October 3, 1973), women defeminize their attire, while men devirilize theirs. The result is not only an inversion of dresses, but also of roles. This exchange gets to the point of "¡Ay, Carlitos, qué bonitos ojos tienes" [My dear, Carlitos, what beautiful eyes you have!]. This exclamation by the male character after dressing in women's clothes shows that dress has the power to change sexual orientation.

Quezada's cartoons are intended to correct vices, in response to the demands of a conservative vision of masculine appearance. Like Posada's works, these also reproach the cross-dressed male body, yet their sense is different. The caricatures designed for the case of the "Cuarenta y uno" communicate scandal and reprobation of a social class through a violation of their private space: that is, for Posada the visibility of what happens in the private realm provokes the reprobation of the transvestite. In Quesada's works, cross-dressing functions as a terrorist action against the virile body. Posada's transvestites belong to the Porfirian oligarchy, educated in Europe in all the delights of fin-de-siècle decadence. In Quesada's works, the cross-dressed speak French, Italian, and English, play golf, and send letters from abroad: they are the children of the postrevolution bourgeoisie. In both, effeminacy means the weakening of national virtues. Hence, effeminacy is incorporated into the discourse of the nation. Association with foreign costumes represents the limit of the national identity. It also represents the limit of virility, as transvestism has been recognized from the fears and temptations produced in a patriarchal hegemony. In the same way we can talk about prostitution and perversions (or the pathology of the "other" sexualities) that have resulted from patriarchal exclusions, cross-dressing has been invented by the patriarchy as an aberration against which virility can be defined.

As the machinery of capitalist society legitimates all the desires that facilitate its operation, according to Deleuze and Guattari, the undesirable objects are established against the grain (60–61). These undesirable objects are not outside the machinery, though; they take part in the process of producing desire. The transvestite is a feared and excluded body in the value system that nationalist artists promote. Nevertheless, because transvestism is useful for establishing the limits of nationality, it takes part in the symbolic universe of nationalism. This fact enables the transvestite to play a contesting role in the drama of the nation. Being denied, he becomes a potential threat; such is his symbolic power.

National Transvestites

Although the transvestite has been explicitly rejected in hegemonic discourse, he has often represented the national by himself without the filter of homophobia. We have already referred to the women cross-dressing in the narratives of the Mexican Revolution. In the media, some effeminate figures were presented as moral and aesthetic arbiters such as Salvador Novo in his capsules in the popular News program *24 Horas con Jacobo Zabludovsky* from the 1960s to his death in 1974, or La Beba Galván of the program *El Güiri Güiri* in TV Azteca, in the late 1980s and early 1990s. Since the 1960s, the popular music band *Los xochimilcas* has been celebrated in the *Teatro Blanquita* for its effeminate performance, and its song "Las mariposas" describing the seduction of a transvestite was a hit.

Since the 1980s, transvestites have been represented in plastic art with the use of dresses full of nationalistic symbols. This appropriation of the national iconography by the effeminate man abolishes the monopoly of virility in the embodiment of the nation. Paintings by Nahum Zenil and Julio Galán, performances by Tito Vasconcelos, and photographs by Graciela Iturbide, among many others, are prominent instances of what Teresa del Conde calls the generation of the neo-Mexicanists (38–39).

In the photograph by Graciela Iturbide entitled "Magnolia" we can see a transvestite wearing a *charro* hat and a nightgown trimmed with lace (see figure 3.2). The subject of the photograph is located off scene, in a corner of daily life. Half-dressed in his intimate space, he stands in slippers on a bare floor in front of a dilapidated, ordinary wall. He is an earthy transvestite stripped of the artifice we observed in Posada, Rivera, Rodríguez Lozano, el Corcito, and Quezada. Nevertheless, he is dressed with the nationalist adornment, the *charro* hat that covers him. All his attire seems appropriate for a transvestite, except for the hat. This added element takes the transvestite beyond his domestic comfort to pose in a stance similar to those in traditional calendar illustrations by Helguera. In fact, he takes a moment to perform a *china poblana*, one of the most popular Mexican *tipos*. But we see a *china poblana* without the colorful skirt and makeup; rather he is a body in the process of cross-dressing, in lingerie. The slippers and the hat introduce a tense contrast. Without the latter, the photograph would not have any visible nationalist intension; with the hat, the entire costume is resignified. The irony is readable as stripping the cross-dresser of his dress and imposing just one nationalist element, the *charro* hat.

Figure 3.2 Gabriela Iturbide *Magnolia*. Courtesy of the artist.

Magnolia is not dressed; he is caught somewhere in-between, en route to the completion of a nationalist transvestite figure. The paint peeling off the wall parallels the precariousness of his attire, establishing a metaphoric connection between scene and dress. Like the wall, the incomplete dress shows the fissures that make evident the masculine body inside the feminine exterior (a double exterior inscribed in the nightgown and the effeminate gesture).

Whether it is a representation in progress or in erosion, the garment of "Magnolia" becomes a differed or in-transit signifier, a sign that is never definitive. Iturbide's photograph of the cross-dressed signifies the deconstruction of the binary gender representation of nation. This deconstruction targets politics of inclusion rather than an antinational manifestation.[1] The recognition of different ways of intramural living such as the intimate cross-dressing life of Magnolia is the subject of a preoccupation we can find in the series *Álbum de familia* by Óscar Sánchez (see figure 3.3). In an interview that took place in 2003, the photographer expresses his intention to show what happens in the daily life of many alternative familiar settings, namely the varying forms of sharing living spaces, which do not conform to the heterosexual couple with children model that the state and religious institutions prescribe. In these pictures, Sánchez goes into the intimate spaces of lesbian couples, friends who share their space and an emotional link, single parents, families, and gay couples with adopted children. Like "Magnolia," these photographs are taken in the private space: the cramped bedrooms that enclose the environment, where touching each other, closing the windows, and lowering one's voice demand to be counted in the records of family rights. The ethnographic accuracy of the intimate field that Sánchez includes in his frame does not need the *charro* hat or *china poblana*'s skirt to signify national identity. Rather than allowing us to see emblems, Óscar Sánchez lets us see the improvised architecture, the tight quarters, and their different versions of love. The exploration of intimacy of the transvestite opens the way to an inquiry into the intimacies of many possibilities, a sort of dissemination of the transvestism beyond the cross-dressing. This is a tendency we can observe in works by Nahum Zenil and Julio Galán, to mention two of the most outstanding painters of the transvestite body.

Figure 3.3   Óscar Sánchez *Claudio y Chantal*. Courtesy of the artist.

Popular Mexican iconography has an inexhaustible source of dresses for the *Escuela Mexicana de Pintura* [The School of Mexican Painting] and the *Neo-Mexicanista* tendency. The garments of saints with the highly encoded colors and forms, the racialized costumes, the traditional puppets, calendars, popular types or stereotypes, and the *lotería* cards (a game similar to Bingo), nurture the performances by Jesusa Rodríguez and Liliana Felipe, Astrid Hadad, and Tito Vasconcelos. There is an iconographic recollection in this neo-Mexicanist art that is reminiscent of the moments of synthesis in the pictorial Mexican tradition: the baroque and the muralist. They do not propose Mexican iconography; they remember and transgress it, misleading and questioning the sense of the nation rather than exalting it. In a sort of tragic irony, national clothing with its implacable festivity dresses painful bodies.

Nahum Zenil's stoic face remains impassive in all his self-portraits. For Zenil, cross-dressing is not about dressing masculine bodies in feminine clothing; nor is it intended to emasculate the political enemy as in Posada, Rivera, and similar artists; rather, the variety of dresses worn by Zenil contrasts with his hard face. Transvestism for Zenil does not mean the stigmatization—or identification—of the transvestite but rather the neutralization of the dress. In his continuous displacement of clothing, his inflexible face carries out a reading of essences that are finally reduced to drags, from which the face of Zenil remains detached.

"Nahum, Nahum, Nahum" represents the many styles of dressing: Nahum as mother, Nahum as sister, Nahum as dog, and so on. They are the reiteration of sameness, pulverizing the self to the point of complete loss of meaning. In the painting *Marcha*, Nahum goes so far as to depict himself repeatedly as part of a multitude attending mass. With these multiplications, transvestism functions in Zenil's works as a machine that designifies both the dresses and the self. This mutual erasure of the body and its attire takes place at the point where the artist's unexpressive and hermetic face explores dress, as he is "seeking identity."

While Graciela Iturbide's photograph erases the nationalist dress by conveying its erosion (or incompleteness); in Zenil's paintings the signs that were originally conferred on the clothes lose their identifying marks to the point of not affecting any aspect of the body they cover. In both, we can observe a resistance to the stigmatization that the transvestism of the masculine body implied in nationalist painting, as we have already pointed out. The erasure of targets neutralizes the difference, and hence the rejection of the transvestite in addition to the derogation of differences.

In the painting "Con tinta sangre de mi corazón" [with my heart's ink-blood], Zenil insists on undifferentiating gender and national dresses. Zenil depicts two characters posing on a proscenium, sharing symmetrically the field of view, both with their hands on their genitals (see figure 3.4). They are dressed as *china poblana* and a *charro* acting on the stage. The fact that they are on the stage suggests the theatrical character of both gender and nation. Those sacred notions are reinterpreted in the performance of a farce. Although this farce recalls the gestures of Posada's transvestites, their belief about representing cross-dressing is radically different. For Posada, the transvestite wears foreign dresses, which identify the national dress code with what is not cross-dressed, while in this piece by Zenil, the transvestite uses the so-called national dress to resignify the nationalist signs. In this way, national expressions can be interpreted because of transvestism. In effect it means that the national consists of imposing dresses; it is constructed by and for appearance. What begins as a reading of the degeneration or deviation from the patriarchy's gender rules valuing virility ends up as a reconfiguration of the nation as nothing more than an external garment. Thus, both gender and nation are nothing but performance.

The works of Julio Galán also explore the redefining and designifying of transvestism and the nation. Like the work of Zenil, most of Galán's work consists of self-portraits and in many cases include neo-Mexicanist iconography with a deconstructive orientation. The title of his painting "Donde ya no hay sexo" [where there is no sex anymore] suggests an indifference to sex-gender. Two characters, both Galán's self-portraits, exhibit signs of saintliness and penitence. One of them is dressed with feminine attire and poses standing in front the spectator, the second one is dressed in masculine clothing upside down. The masculine character, smaller than the effeminate one, is bleeding and holds thorny

Figure 3.4 Nahum Zenil *Con tinta sangre de mi corazón* [with bloody ink of my heart]. Courtesy of the artist and the Galería de Arte Mexicano.

branches in his hands. The effeminate character is dressed up in Christian symbols and has long hair with a halo around his head. On his chest, there is a cross and his left hand points to his heart as in the Sacred-Heart icon. His right hand points upward. The title of the piece is inscribed on this cross-dressed character. Next to his left hand, there is a vase with roses. A stairwell located down behind the vase and the cloudy sky in the background represent the escapes that we can see in works by Enrique Guzmán, an immediate precursor of this neo-Mexicanist group, whose iconoclastic view and anguish are continuously reproduced in Galán's and Zenil's works. This piece by Galán links Christian imagery to transvestism resulting in the desexualizing of the human body. It is difficult to find an ironic wink or even a utopian vision of pregenital sexuality, as Rudy C. Bleys suggests, about this painting (127). On the contrary, the desexualization is painful: this and other bloody representations by Galán imply a dramatic castration. Sacred dresses exercise violence on Galán's body. Therefore, the manner of dress is not just an illusory transfiguration of identity, but also a process of eliminating any sexuality.

The painting "Niño embarazado" [pregnant child] by Galán leads the viewer's gaze beyond the subject's dresses, to the emptiness that the dress wraps. This can be interpreted as an inner transvestism, although this expression seems impossible. The process of cross-dressing has overcome the surface clothing. The child with manicured nails and rouged lips that we find in many works by Galán, points to his bulky stomach, which is denied by the inscription at the left "dentro de mí tú no estás" [you are not inside me]. The addressee of this inscription remains unknown. It is an open text, that is, its meaning may disseminate toward any possible "you" that, in addition, is not there. This emptiness invites an infinite reconstruction of the sense of cross-dressing. From the violent desexualization of the castrated to the exhaustion of the interior, Julio Galán offers a negative approach to interpreting transvestism: it consists not of signifying the body, but stripping it of any subjectivity.

The piece entitled "La tehuana" is, among Galán's works, the one that has probably gone too far in the representation of transvestism. It is the representation of the pure dress without a face; in an etymological sense, it is a depersonalization (lacking face). In place of a face there is a hole in which—like in the certain panels of popular photographs—anybody can pose. The painting then is nothing but a dress to be worn by the public. That is, the painting is something to be worn as well as something in which to be seen. The progressive erasure of the subject we have seen in "Donde no hay sexo" and "Niño embarazado" has culminated in its total disappearance.

The representation of the transvestite body in Mexican art conveys the use of masculine images as political actions. For the most socially accepted view, transvestism functions as a means of emasculating the ideological opposite, which is understood as losing maleness by losing one's virile appearance. From the cartoons in the nineteenth century-journalism to those by Abel Quezada of cold war PRI (*Partido Revolucionario Institucional*) era, we can observe that popular images of cross-dressing reflect the misogynist and homophobic consensus, which presents the transvestite as an enemy of the nation. On the other hand, it is also a political representation of effeminacy in the postrevolutionary art (Abraham Ángel, Tebo, and Rodíguez Lozano, among others) in terms of the affirmation of a homosexual identity. In the neo-Mexicanist art (Nahum Zenil, Graciela Iturbide, and Julio Galán), transvestism represents a deconstruction of the homophobic view we have seen in the Porfiriato's popular art and the *Escuela Mexicana de Pintura*, precisely by nationalizing cross-dressing. Finally, we can observe that, as a consequence of this deconstructive process of recent years, transvestism connotes a blurring of gender identity distinctions, either by the multiplication of dresses—which implies that identity is exchangeable—or by the disappearance of the subject, suggesting that identity is a question of surfaces.

Part 2

The Homosocial Passions

4

Intimacy in the War:
The Revolutionary Desire

Many of the narratives that have shaped the public's vision of the Mexican Revolution have been paradigmatic in constructing the idea of a national masculinity. To narrate the civil war saga is also to recognize the fundamental significance of the heroic men who shaped the national project in the postrevolutionary era. Description of the relationship between revolutionary men in these stories leads to the analysis of the homosocial bond as an intimate system that structures the power relations engendering the state. My reading of the novel *El águila y la serpiente* (1928 [The Eagle and the Snake]) by Martín Luis Guzmán seeks to describe this intimate system. The second part of this chapter revisits controversies about the construction of a national culture that took place in Mexico City during the 1920s and 1930s. I intend to explain how the Mexican state claims to become a virile institution by expelling effeminacy, and by dressing public issues—that is, the revolutionary state—with gender signification. Although homophobia defines the national project, homosocial behaviors are described as male-to-male affection, and effeminacy plays an important role in the construction of the Mexican revolutionary state. The strategies for keeping this homosocial bond contained within homophobic limits are crucial for understanding Mexican masculinity in this period.

Lovely Beasts: Masculine intimacy in
El águila y la serpiente by Martín Luis Guzmán

En route to Sonora, Mexico, where they would join the forces of the *División del Norte*, Martín Luis Guzmán and Alberto Pani stopped in San Antonio, Texas, where José Vasconcelos received them at the main train station with euphoric cries to celebrate the triumph of Francisco "Pancho" Villa in Ciudad Juárez against the Federal Army: "Now we won! Now we have a real man!" (Guzmán 35). The military success of the mythic warrior, Villa, is the subject of a myriad of historical narratives intended to make visible the symbolic fabric that forms the revolutionary nation. In their epic enthusiasm crowned with slogans that incited the masses to punish public enemies, revolutionary discourses dress masculine bodies with a series of virtues. These instead of referring to rebel values, materialize in a sort of bellicose eroticism that translates military skills into a body that seduces, attacks, and penetrates, as we see repeatedly in the descriptions of battle scenes in all the novels of the revolution. *El águila y la serpiente* is an autobiographical journey of Martín Luis Guzmán that begins with his escape from Mexico City after the assassination of the president, Francisco I. Madero. Guzmán travels with Alberto Pani from Veracruz to Havana, Cuba, and then to New Orleans. They proceed to join the Revolutionary Army in northern Mexico. The novel is constructed as a truthful account of the political and military activities of the *División del Norte* from its first battles in Ciudad Juárez (1911) to its fragmentation and the defeat of Pancho Villa (1915). Guzmán collaborates with Pancho Villa for most of this journey until he is forced to abandon Villa after his defeat by Obregón.

Vasconcelos' exclamation to his surprised visitors in the San Antonio train station proclaims that historical justice is achieved, while the nation is materialized or imagined as a body that the hero possesses erotically. "Now we have a real man" is a phrase that conveys a mythic eroticism capable of giving birth to the motherland. Far from understanding these images as rhetorical prudery, I would like to underline the enthusiasm displayed by Vasconcelos and his visitors as an example of heroic eroticism. In *El águila y la serpiente* in which this anecdote is narrated, an autobiographical narrator presents us with an intimate view of the battlefield scene. For this novel, to narrate the revolution is to narrate the contact between male bodies that gives birth to the nation.[1] We observe an emotional exchange in the gaze shared by the male characters, a gaze that is more than an allegory for the nation. The narrator in *El águila y la serpiente* intends to present us with the image of the hero as a desirable body, a body composed by the gaze that euphorically venerates the great men of the nation. While critics have often spoken of bestowing a pious look on a sacred icon, this gaze, by contrast, exalts the virile attributes of the heroes and therefore eroticizes their veneration.

> Pani admiraba ya a Obragón y se sentía atraído por el temple autoritario del Primer Jefe. Por Obregón, desde luego, su simpatía era tanta que de él llevaba entonces en la cartera un retrato en tarjeta postal . . . y a menudo, rebosante de sincero patriotismo, lo sacaba para mirarlo, mientras decía:
> —Con tres hombres así, ¿a dónde llegaría México? (35–36)

> [Pani admired Obregón already and he felt attracted to the first general's authoritative composure. In fact, such was his sympathy toward Obregón that he kept in his wallet a postcard portrait of him . . . and often, full of sincere patriotism, he contemplated it, while saying:
> —with three men like this, how far would Mexico go?]

Pani's veneration of Obregón places the small portrait alongside the symbol of the nation. Guzmán presents the motherland as the destiny of his enthusiasm and Obregón's image as the element that mediates between Pani and the nation. The tropic relationship between Obregón and the nation establishes the authoritative image that explains Vasconcelos' exclamation, "Now we have a real man" that, at the lexical level, eroticizes the relationship between heroes and those who signify them as such.

For Bakhtin, the narrator's gaze embraces the hero (13) or, to use a parallel metaphor, the construction of the hero's meaning depends on the voice that focuses on him. The hero's exteriority defines his status as object of desire. Hence becoming a hero is possible, thanks to the gaze that represents him. The mechanism we can observe in the construction of Obregón's heroic image allows us to recognize similarly that the desire for the hero is the desire for his authority as it is inscribed in the portrait stashed in Pani's wallet. The concept of the nation appears, then, as a way to replace fascination with virility. It is an allegorical recourse that reestablishes the essence, that is, the national idea, before homophobia turns Pani's veneration into guilt.

Desire for the virile is suspended before arriving at its consummation; it is then a desire interrupted by homophobic panic. Therefore, the gender norm that contextualizes *El águila y la serpiente* has to be understood in terms of a homophobic nation. From this conception, any erotic suggestion in the description of the masculine body has to be constrained, resulting in the nationalization of eroticism, and in the translation of the hero's body into the abstract notion of the nation, as we can see in phrases such as, "retozaban los misteriosos resortes de la nacionalidad" (40). [The mysterious springs of nationality romped.] or "el corazón iba bailándonos de gozo conforme las raíces de nuestra alma encajaban como en algo conocido, tratado y amado durante siglos" (40). [The heart danced inside us with joy as the roots of our soul penetrated something familiar that we have lived for centuries.] Such expressions reflect some of Pani's and Vaconcelos' feelings as they cross the Río Bravo (the Rio Grande River) from El Paso to Ciudad Juárez on their way to interview Francisco Villa. In this encounter with the nation, the verb "to romp" and the joyful penetration felt by the narrator slide us back to the semantic field of eroticism. The slippage begins in the erotization of the hero's body and ends in the erotization of the nation's body, thus completing a circle of transfigurations in which hero and nation are juxtaposed in the same desiring action.

The description of the body as a tactile presence allows intimate moments between men. The homosociety of revolutionary men remains at the threshold of enjoyment, never named but always apparent merely as a sensory event. When they arrive in the room where Villa receives them, the character and narrator Martín Luis Guzmán describes the encounter as follows: "yo, a invitación del guerrillero, me había sentado ya en el borde del catre, a un dedo del cuerpo que lo ocupaba. El calor de aquel lecho penetró mi ropa y me llegó a la carne" (45). [After the guerilla warrior invited me to do so, I sat on the edge of his camp bed, just one finger's length away from his body. The heat of that bed penetrated my clothes and touched my flesh.]

While Obregón's portrait instigates a process of allegorization that ends in the eroticization of both, the hero and the nation, this encounter with Villa, the concrete carnal hero, does not seem to offer any rhetorical escape into emblem. It is a materialized body that is desired and feared at the same time, a body whose meaning fluctuates between admiration and danger. Therefore the narrator describes the guerilla fighter as a "jaguar a quien pasábamos la mano acariciadora por el lomo, temblando de que nos tirara un zarpazo" (46). [A jaguar over whose back we passed our caressing hand, trembling with fear that he might claw us.] This feared and desired body creates a threshold that suspends desire without consummating it. Vasconcelos's phrase, "now we have a real man" comes back to Gúzman's mind, after this interview with Francisco Villa, except that this time it comes without the allegorical filter of the nation. Instead, Villa's body is placed in the liminality between eroticism and politics that defines desire in this novel.

This narrative liminality provides at the same time a moment of erotization, an escape from the hero's body into allegory (as we see in Pani's veneration of Obregón), as well as a space of danger and attraction (as in the interview with Villa). In both cases we observe the construction of a strategy to avoid the consummation of erotic desire. This provides the narrative of El águila y la serpiente with an economy that produces an infinite and allegorized desire for the hero, as in the deviant's interminable search for the object of desire which he never possesses and for which, moreover, he never professes a desire per se. To name a desire of the hero's body would only open the way to the opposite movement: its abjection and condemnation. Therefore, to linger within the liminality of desire is a condition that stays within the frame of social law that imposes homophobia as a necessary condition for national hygiene.

To name sexuality, as it is understood in the proclamations of sexual-identity politics since the last half of the twentieth century, is to define bodies according to private practices whose exposure the heterosexual dominant norm prohibits. From that dividing line onward, classifications such as homosexual, lesbian, bisexual, transexual, and transgender have been produced as positions from which to fight for respect for alternative life styles. *El águila y la serpiente* hardly proposes male bodies as sexual identities; rather it slides them underneath any definition. They are constituted by practices that escape denomination, constructing what Marjorie Garber calls "Latin bisexuality," which refers to homoerotic practices between men who consider themselves heterosexuals (30). Instead of defining themselves in the field of alternative identities (which at the time of the novel, were practically nonexistent), the desire for the hero expressed here seems to contribute to the consolidation of the virile image; thus we have to read it as a virilizing homophilia rather than as politics of excluded groups.

Villa's escape from the jail of San Pedro Tlatelolco is one of the episodes of the novel that is most relevant to this homophilic attraction to the hero. Carlitos Jáuregui (who after the episode became Villa's assistant), met the guerrilla fighter in court when he was transcribing Villa's testimony. Jáuregui describes this encounter to Guzmán as follows: "[l]o que sí conservaba idéntico era el toque de ternura que asomaba a sus ojos [Villa's] cuando me veía. Esa mirada que se grabó en mí de modo inolvidable, la descubrí desde la primera ocasión en que el juez me encargó de asentar en el expediente las declaraciones que Villa iba haciendo" (164). [What remained identical was the touch of tenderness that came from his eyes when he looked at me. I first discovered that look that became unforgettably engraved in me the first time that the judge charged me with transcribing Villa's declarations.] After a few days behind bars, Villa inquired about Jáuregui's sad expression and promised to take him away from his sad circumstances. Jáuregui visited Villa every day and could not even sleep for worrying that he would not be able to correspond with him. In the whole episode, a double discourse makes visible, and at the same time conceals, an attraction between Villa and Jáuregui. The glances and affective expressions from Villa to Jáuregui, who is addressed in the diminutive throughout the novel, begin the framework of escape from which an intimate relationship takes off, although it is defined by terms such as loyalty and solidarity that are in the service of the revolutionary war.

In *Memorias de Pancho Villa* (1960) a biography also written by Martín Luis Guzmán, Pancho Villa's voice speaks of the same period in which Jáuregui frequently visited the prison, as follows:

> Yo seguí yendo a verlo al juzgado cuando calculaba encontrarlo solo . . . y Carlitos siguió visitándome en mi cuarto. Así se acrecentaron nuestras ligas de amistad, y de ese modo, cuando ya le había dado yo espontáneamente más de quinientos pesos, con ánimo de que me cogiera cariño, estuve cierto de la lealtad suya y de su desinterés. (*Memorias* . . . 160–161)

> [I kept going to see him at the court room when I thought I could find him there alone . . . and Carlitos [Jáuregui] kept visiting me in my room. In that way our bonds of friendship grew, and for that reason, when I had given him more than 500 pesos spontaneously, with the intention of garnering his affection; I was assured of his loyalty and of his honesty.]

In the frequent visits that have the express intention of preparing an escape from the prison, the development of an intimate affection is evidenced by phrases such as "to increase our bonds of friendship" or "to garner his affection." In the following pages, Villa interrogates Carlitos about women finally in Toluca after the escape:

> ¿Y qué tal es usted para las muchachas, amiguito?
> ¿Para las muchachas, mi general?
> Sí, amiguito: para las muchachas.
> No sé mi general.
> Pues ahora lo vamos a saber.
> (*Memorias* . . . 170)

> [And what are your skills with women, little friend?
> With women, my general?
> Yes, little friend: with women.
> I don't know, my general.
> Well now we are going to find out.]

Villa's questions disclose that Carlitos Jáuregui has had no sexual experience with women. Villa suspects that he is a novice. In this dialogue we do not see any reproach about this failure but a sort of sponsorship of Jáuregui's initiation into the virile duties. The question "And how are your skills with women, little friend?" refers to sexual experience with women, as if it were a physical virtue such as being a good horse rider or a good runner. In that sense, the relationship with women in Villa's virile universe—at least the one we can see in this interrogatory—can be explained as an erotic competence rather than an affection that began and developed in the field of friendship, loyalty, and caring. Nevertheless asking about erotic skills can also be interpreted as a sexual insinuation.

Francisco Villa appears to his biographers' eyes as a man inclined to affection, rather than as the cruel revolutionary constructed by the narratives of his detractors. Although Friedrich Katz—the most renowned historiographer specialized on Villa's revolution—reduces the importance of Carlitos Jáuregui's role and does not mention the affective relationship that contextualizes the episode of the escape, his work includes many references to Villa's affective expressions as he addresses his troops, and even his enemies, in almost all his letters, interviews, and other documents reporting his statements. He addresses his army as "my boys whom I love a lot" (Katz I, 217); in his letters to president Madero, who put him in jail—even though he was one of the key warriors in the Maderista revolution—his last statement is "with affection and respect as always" (Katz 1: 215). The norms of loyalty that we observe in the relationship among revolutionaries display a homosociality constructed through affective pacts rather than a military morality, to such an extent that we can speak of intimate friendships and loving complicities.

Even though there is no declaration in the novel *El águila y la serpiente* that could lead us to a definition of homoerotic relationships, men's bodies are described as attractive to the eyes of the (male) narrator. In fact, this gaze is so focused on male bodies that its descriptive principles may well belong to the category of erotic aesthetics. Although the physical presence of the hero reinforces his virtues as a leader in this intended epic narrative, we can also observe an eroticization of the epic text. In this way, in the scene where the revolutionary soldiers dance with the women from

Magdalena, Sonora, some of the leaders of the *División del Norte*
are described as follows:

> Enrique C. Llorente no se cansaba a esa hora de seguir haciendo
> estragos con sus grandes bigotes inflexibles y la hermosa onda de su
> cabellera—"ala de cuervo"—que coronaba tan bien su gentil figura.
> Martínez Alomía demostraba andando que la languidez tropical y
> costeña se ensamblaba a maravilla con el brío preciso del norte. Rafael
> Zurbarán, con su habla fácil e insinuante, con sus modales perfectos,
> con su sutil ironía, no encontraba barreras. (65)

> [Enrique C. Llorente was restlessly wreaking havoc with his inflexible
> mustache and the wave of his hair—"wing of a raven"—that crowned
> very well his gentlemanly figure. Martínez Alomía showed in his move-
> ments that the tropical and coastal listlessness assimilated perfectly to
> the precise verve of the north. Rafael Zurbarán, with his smooth and
> suggestive speech, his correct manners, and his subtle irony, had no
> barriers].

"Wreaking havoc with the mustache and hair," "the assimilation
of the coastal listlessness with the verve of the north," and "the
suggestive speech against which there is no barrier" are phrases
that describe the seductive dynamics of these men. While the male
characters are brought into focus with such suggestive details,
females are mentioned as cute or attractive, without the meticulous
attention that male bodies receive.

General Rodolfo Fierro is one of the characters more expan-
sively considered in the novel. An American journalist has
described him as a "beautiful beast" (354), and has said that his
"verbal sweetness" (353) could persuade Guzmán to give him
any favor that he asked:

> [u]na mañana Rodolfo Fierro llegó a la Secretaría de Guerra menos
> compuesto que de costumbre. En realidad su hermosa figura se con-
> servaba íntegra. Llevaba como siempre aquel admirable par de mitasas
> que adquirían en sus piernas un vigor de línea extraordinario. (354)

> [One morning, Rodolfo Fierro arrived at the War Office less well-turned
> out than usual. However, his beautiful figure was not affected. He wore
> as always that admirable pair of pants that gave his legs an extraordinary
> line of vigor.]

His description follows:

> [a]llí, cruzadas las piernas bellas y hercúleas, puesto el codo sobre la
> rodilla, inclinado el busto hacia la mano, mientras los dedos maceraban
> el rollo de tabaco y la boca despedía humo, cobraba su carácter preciso,
> su luz propia, su irradiación exacta.
>
> [There he crossed his beautiful Hercules' legs, with his elbow on his
> knee, and his chest inclined toward his hand while his finger macerated
> the slug of tobacco and his mouth exhaled smoke, he acquired a precise
> character, his own light, even his own radiance.]

The characterization, the dress, the posture, and those adjectives
that emphasize admiration provide the hero with a body to be
looked at. The character poses for the seduced gaze of the narrator.
Although he is an objectified body, his active posing and modula-
tion of his voice show that he is participating actively in this aesthetic game as a subject that is attracting admiration; that is, he is
a seducer subject. This encounter between the hero's body and the
narrator's gaze allows us to propose a deviation from eroticism to
textual production. Desire is translated into a verbal economy—
the production of textual bodies that are going to ornament the
history of the nation.

Nevertheless, this ornamentation manages to divert attention
away from its decorative function; regardless of the interest it gar-
ners by association with the nation's narrative, it is itself an ero-
tized masculine body, as we have already analyzed in the depiction
of Indians by Saturnino Herrán in chapter 1. The ornament, the
parergon, that is, the frame of the artistic object disassociated from
its content, conveys the disinterested idea of aesthetics proposed by
Kant in his *Critique of Judgment* (46–50). However, in Derrida's
reading of the Kantian aesthetics, the emphasis on the supplementary elements, as opposed to the content, takes us out of the artistic work, that is out of its intentionality and thus, the text
overcomes all the limits that it originally had imposed (Derrida
258). Next, this divergence opens the way to an implicit interest
and rather than to mere Kantian purism. By allowing ourselves to
focus on the way the narrator gazes on masculine bodies instead of
paying attention to the war plot, we try to escape from the text's
intentionality by way of the ornamental description. Ultimately, we

do not find the emptiness of an ambiguous game of representations on the exterior of the bodies but actively opt for a reading of eroticism as a fundamental element in the dynamics of bodies that constitute the national imagination beyond the war plot. Out of the fabric of the diegesis—the story of how men constructed the nation—we focus on the fabric of the corporeal and find that the masculine body is the most visible form of the national.

Novels of the revolution, muralist paintings, the poetry of *Los contemporáneos* group, and the essays that reflect on national identity starting from the 1930s, as well as Mexican cinema of the so-called Golden Age reiterate this intimate relationship between the nation and the representation of male bodies, as this book shows.

How is it possible to associate male eroticism with the nation in the definition of aesthetics? If the novel of the revolution represents the earlier process that constructs the national culture, the novel represents the nation as a romance, an eroticized narrative, which according to Doris Sommer, is evident when fiction includes metaphors such as to germinate, to conceive, and to procreate the nation (30–51). To germinate a new society, in Sommer's reading of nineteenth century Latin American fiction, is a heterosexual project, overwhelmed by a sentimental mood. Meanwhile in the narratives of the Mexican revolution—of which *El águila y la serpiente* is one of the most paradigmatic instances—we may underline a drastically different form of romance—a homophilia continuously restrained by homophobia. The circle of seduction and repression reveals a contradiction that provides the meaning of the national hero: in this phallocentric society, the male body claims its centrality as the hero figure; this centrality makes his body an object of desire. On the other hand, if virility is prestigious, effeminacy is dishonorable. To become effeminate, in this system of erotic-aesthetic values, means to lose the most precious value. Thus, losing one's virility means losing one's nationality: that is why just by being an object of desire, the decorative male bodies in *El águila y la serpiente* place virility at the center of national aesthetics.

Intimacy in *El águila y la serpiente* escapes homophobic judgment through silence under which the body seems to act without constraints. The gazes and the touches have not been coded as signs of nefarious sin but as forms of leisure comparable to vice, partying, and racketeering as Núñez Noriega describes it in his ethnographic work on northern Mexico (209–210). The hordes of revolutionaries seem to devote themselves blindly to the excitation stimulated only by swinging between danger and euphoria. Martín Luis Guzmán attends one of the massive parties organized by General Carrasco during the occupation of Culiacán. He arrives, when the street is dark, and

tropecé con algo—al parecer con las piernas de un cuerpo recostado contra la pared—y me fui de bruces hacia el lodo. Pero al extender los brazos en el curso de la caída, mis manos, abiertas en anticipación del suelo, dieron milagrosamente en la ropa de otro cuerpo, al que me agarré. Este segundo cuerpo estaba a pie firme, según noté en seguida, y fue a sus piernas a lo que me mantuve asido mientras mi rodillas se posaban en el lodo con fresca blandura. Mi salvador invisible pareció entender lo que me pasaba, pues sentí una mano fuerte que me cogía por la axila, que me ayudaba a enderezarme y que, por último, me soltaba un instante para convertirse en brazo echado sobre mis hombros, brazo cariñoso, brazo que me apretaba el cuello con inesperado afecto, sensación que se desvaneció en mí en el acto para resolverse en la de un olor humano desagradabilísimo y a vueltas con el tufo del mezcal. Entonces hice un vigoroso movimiento para soltarme de aquel cuerpo que se me juntaba; pero como el brazo me sujetó con mayor fuerza, y al mismo tiempo una puerta de la acera de enfrente dejó escapar un rayo de luz, me torné inmóvil. El que me abrazaba dijo: —¡Anda, pos y que te me queres ir! (95–96)

[I ran over something—it seemed that the legs of a body leaned against the wall—and fell flat on my face into the mud. But when I extended my arms while falling, my hands, opened before I hit the ground, met the clothes of someone else, which I grabbed. This second body was standing firmly, as I noticed immediately. I kept grabbing his legs while my knees lodged in the soft, fresh mud. My invisible rescuer seemed to understand what had happened to me, because I felt his strong hand lift me under my armpit to help me get up and finally release me for a second to put his arm around my shoulders, a loving arm, an arm that firmly touched my neck with an unexpected affection. This sensation vanished very soon to be replaced by a very disgusting human odor mixed with the stench of mezcal. Then I made a vigorous movement to get free of that body that was attached to me; but as his arm held me with more strength and at the same time a door from across the street let through a ray of light, I grew still. The one who hugged me said, "So, you want to run away from me!"]

For more than two hours, this stranger held Guzmán. As in the case of the Jáuregui and Villa relationship, the corporeal activity takes place in the darkness of the indefinite. It is a pure corporeality in which due to the clumsiness of their inebriated state, signs are articulated through accidental actions and they elude consciousness. In this delirious juxtaposition of the two bodies, we can find the symbolic negotiation between homophobia and male-to-male desire, the two faces of the masculine that construct the epic of the revolution. Darkness hides the man who rescues Guzmán from falling in the mud. The "loving arm" of the rescuer keeps touching him with an unexpected affection, but is immediately rejected with repulsion. Guzmán notices a disgusting odor that parallels the affection of the unknown man. The text is ambiguous about this rejection: it is at the same time a physical repulsion because of the odor, and a fear of the affection expressed by the "loving arm" that kept touching him. The exclamation "so, you want to run away from me!" by this man makes clear his homoerotic intention, and therefore, he is rejected for keeping homophobic norms.

This scene of Culiacán suggests that machismo and homoeroticism do not necessarily exclude each other when we speak of Mexican male homosociety. However, this statement must be developed further as we analyze the function of homophobia in the genesis of a postrevolutionary culture. Narratives that refrain from advancing beyond the description of semiaccidental touching or that involve a gaze that suggests desire without revealing a homoerotic attraction clearly show that homophobia works in the interstices of descriptions without definitions.

Feminizing the Revolution

The presentation of the male-to-male relationship in an ambiguous discourse saturates the representation not only of bodies but also of the nation itself, as we can see in the various works that we consider in this book. Homophobia is articulated in terms of the limits between what is and is not the national. Revolutionary homophobia expresses a rejection of forms and discourses that connote imperialist influence; for example, the "French" mannerism of the elite in the Profirio Díaz regime characterizes one type of the antinational. In the postrevolutionary era, homophobia becomes a political position that fundamentally manifests public discourse. Feminization shows the political enemy in the dominated position, a compromise which can be read as a sexualization of power relationships (Bourdieu 2000, 35–36).

The erosion of the masculine body, from the scandal of "the ball of the 41" to *El águila y la serpiente*, is one of the most prominent features of the political discourses of emancipation. "The ball of the 41" represents Mexican political and economical dependency on imperialism by exposing the weakness of the leading class. The scandal produced a disempowerment and symbolized a defeat of the dominator, using the sexual metaphor on which Octavio Paz and Pierre Bourdieu concur. Visible effeminacy nurtures public discourses that overlay the national in the first three decades of the twentieth century. The problem of virility and effeminacy, in terms of gendered images that represent political notions such as nationality, dependency, and emancipation, inform the whole process of the Mexican revolution.

In 1925 and again in 1932, the newspapers in Mexico City published a number of articles as part of a large and complex controversy about revolutionary culture, virility and effeminacy.[2] Rather than insisting on Manichean discussions that present irreconcilable positions, we may conceive, by paying attention to the literary and artistic works produced in the midst of these polemics, a constant intersection between virility and homophilia that reduces polarizations and explains the contradictions already embedded in the construction of Mexican male images. Right away, we notice that heterosexual homophobic subjects are not alone in expressing their antihomosexual discourse, as it also appears in texts by self-defined homosexuals; in these texts the homophobic references soften hostile attacks in addition to subduing the machista order. Such self-denigration opens the way to the realization that homosexual discourse constantly includes homophobic statements. Homophobia exists as a social discourse, as a citation that overcomes its own intentionality. Several texts by Salvador Novo,

Xavier Villaurrutia, and Elías Nandino present a tension between desire and abjection, a permitted way of being themselves in the social arena, where citation is a prior condition to making sense (Butler 1997, 33).

On the topic of intersection, I want to emphasize that the construction of what can be called national aesthetics could be explained in terms of transfigurations that happen despite (and because of) the polarization that pervades the controversies of the 1920s and 1930s. The notion of homosexuality as a disease and the fear of being infected by it are the most common statements in the arguments by those who propose that the nation should be virile (meaning homophobic). In both the 1925 and 1932 controversies, homosexuality is described as a social decadence, a highly infectious disease, and a compromise of the virility that affects the strength of revolutionary institutions.[3] The idea of contamination, which was part of the fears that constituted the socialist/nationalist morals of most revolutionary artists and intellectuals of the period, saturates the arguments in favor of a virile state that we can read in several newspaper articles published about these controversies. The artists and intellectuals thought that it was imperative to prevent the state from the disease of effeminacy in public life and in literature (which is the place where the nation is imagined).

In February 1925 in an article entitled "Miseria del hombre de letras" [the Misfortune of the Man of Letters], Julio Jiménez Rueda states, "La vida burocrática mata en el intelectual toda virilidad, por eso los eunucos abundan en las oficinas... la literatura se empequeñece y afemina" (cit. in Díaz Arciniegas 115). [Bureaucratic life kills all virility in intellectuals, that's why eunuchs crowd the offices . . . literature diminishes and effeminizes them.] The idea of effeminacy corresponds to the lack of nationalism, the absence of social commitment as well as historical consciousness. The state representatives decree the virility of literature in those terms. When José Manuel Puig Casauranc was appointed director of the Office of Public Education, he affirmed in his inaugural speech that his administration "ayudará a la divulgación de toda obra mexicana en que la decoración amanerada de una falsa comprensión esté substituida por la otra decoración, hosca y severa, y a veces fría pero siempre cierta de nuestra vida misma" (cit. in Díaz Arciniegas

89) [he would support the distribution of every Mexican work that substitutes mannerist decoration and false comprehension with decoration that is sullen, severe, and sometimes cold, but always certain of our life, as such.] The state's discourse establishes that mannerism implies a false comprehension; it is deceiving and antinational, whereas the national is characterized in aesthetic and gender terms—as virile, and then virility associated with the words "sullen" and "realistic." In fact those adjectives will be used to define three of the aesthetic models associated with the revolutionary state: the Mexican School of Painting (in which muralism is the most prominent expression), the group of poets called *estridentistas* (a sort of futuristic and socially oriented movement), and the novels of the revolution.

The nationalistic aesthetics, by distinguishing itself as realist and virile, opens the way to the categorization of artistic forms in a binary logic: realistic versus fantastic; virile versus effeminate; sullen versus mannerist. With these binaries, national characteristics will acquire the greatest value. It is not precisely the heterosexual norm, but virile nationalism that imposes the criterion for valorizing aesthetic expressions, and thus, gender attributes dominate the political hegemony and control the public sphere. According to Casauranc, the feminine and effeminacy are expelled from the national aesthetic project. Does this mean that visible masculinity and masculinization are the only authorized aesthetic expressions? Women who participate in the intellectual and artistic life of the postrevolutionary period conform to this norm as they are perceived and constructed as virile figures. Such are the cases of Gabriela Mistral and Frida Khalo, two female individuals with a high public visibility.[4]

Salvador Novo is the public persona most exposed to the eyes of the intellectuals who defended the virility of the state. Besides being one of the most caustic satirists of 1920s to 1970s, his body became an icon that represented the effeminacy execrated from the aesthetic politics of the revolution. Paintings by Manuel Rodríguez Lozano, Diego Rivera, Antonio Ruiz El Corcito, and others who depicted Novo, deserve a lengthier consideration than we had given them in the previous chapter. Doubtlessly Novo is the character described in the article "Por el ojo de la llave. Literatura y bilis" [through the lock. Literature and bile] by an anonymous author, published on May 23, 1932 in the Newspaper *El Universal*: "Entonces los literatos, ojerosos y exangües, son más nerviosos que nunca. Se polvean y murmuran los unos a los otros. Se depilan las cejas y desuellan al colega. Y no desaprovechan jamás la ocasión de lanzar pullas, pasando la punta de meñique manicurado por los labios para emparejar el color" (cit. in Sheridan 230–231). [Thus, the literati, haggard and weakened, are more nervous than ever. They preen themselves and gossip against the others; they pluck their eyebrows and skin their colleagues alive. Never wasting the occasion to insult, they fix the color of the lipstick with a mani-cured finger.] The artificiality of the cosmetics contrasts with the frank roughness of the virile type. The themes deployed in letters, manifestos, editorial opinions, and brief, clarifying notes, endlessly associate effeminacy with the European influence, the *non-estridentista* avant-gardes (i.e., the avant-garde nonrevolutionary aesthetics practiced by the purist writers), and the universalist posi-tion. This effeminacy is presented as a social illness that weakens revolutionary culture and as a colonialist posture that works against the nation.

Lacking the virile attributes expected by the dominant voices of the revolutionary state, the other avant-garde, the group of *Contemoráneos* magazine, remains excluded from the official aesthetics; thus in 1934 it was quite acceptable to demand that the members of this group be removed from any public service position, because of "su dudosa condición psicológica" (cit. in Balderston 62). [their doubtful psychological condition.] One of the writers who signed a request for this exclusion was José Rubén Romero, a novelist of the revolution. Although he proclaims the virile revolution while participating in controversies about national culture, some of the protagonists of his novels are effeminate. In his novel *Apuntes de un lugareño* [Notes by a Village Man] the narra-tor describes Gabino, a salesclerk in a grocery store in a village, as a "tipo afeminado, de andares zarandeadores, pleitero contumaz con todas las comadres del barrio y que, como una mujer, se cobi-jaba con un chal a cuadros y fumaba sosteniéndose un codo con la otra mano" (54). [an effeminate type, with shaking gait, stubborn, aggressive with all women in the neighborhood and that, like a woman, he wore a checkered shawl and smoked sustaining his elbow with his other hand.] Nevertheless, this character leads the discussions in a group that gathers every evening in his country store, the only place where people read literary works and could be informed of political events. Hypocritically, while Romero requests the expulsion of effeminate intellectuals from official service, in his novel the effeminate character performs the role of spreading revolutionary ideals. Gabino's intellectual revolution contrasts with the revolution as war. Instead of describing the battlefield, the usual site in the novel of the revolution where homosocial relationships develop—as we saw in Martín Luis Guzmán's work—in Romero's novels, life remains in the quotidian routine of the rural environment. Whereas the extraordinary situation of the war could explain the emergence of homoerotic contacts in novels as those of Guzmán, in the quietness of *Apuntes de un lugareño*, the homosexual character is already preestablished. It is arguable whether Gabino belongs to a social typology, a suggestion that provides this novel with *costumbrista* features. In contrast with the intolerance that Romero expresses in real life against the *Contemporaneos* group, in his novels Romero takes a more tolerant stance. He does not consider Gabino, an ill or antisocial character, as is evident from the leading role that Romero assigns him.

In another novel by Romero, *Desvandada* [Escape], a single man, who is also a salesclerk in a grocery store and who likes to play in the river with the village teenagers, narrates his own story (148). In this case, the character is not effeminate like Gabino, but he is also the leader of opinion when neighbors gather. An ideological character, he proclaims political ideas that support the revolution. At the end of the novel, the revolutionary hordes invade the village and the cowardly salesclerk hides in the church with the women. If the homosexual character emits revolutionary ideas and if violence is not considered revolutionary—the most ideological character of the novel escapes violence—then virility does not necessarily define revolution in the perspective of the novel. This contradiction opens the way to suggest that criticism of the revolution is based on criticism of virile violence. The role of nonvirile characters in leading the intelligentsia in the countryside is a theme that we can find in various novels of the revolution. Cowardly, ambiguous, and weak characters contrast with heroes whose illiterate aggressiveness stages the spectacle of destruction.

Unfocused violence, without a solid ideological articulation, is the form of heroism in most of the novels of the revolution. Such is the case in novels such as *Los de abajo* by Mariano Azuela, *Se llevaron el cañón para Bachimba* by Felipe Muñoz, or *Tropa vieja* by Francisco L. Urquizo, to mention a few of the many examples. In the last, nonvirile characters are absent although most of the novel is located in military seclusion. According to the narrator, the introduction of women in the military base explains the absence of homoeroticism.

> Dicen que más antes no entraban las mujeres aquí y que en el rancho echaban alcanfor y quién sabe qué otras tarugadas para que a la gente no le diera ganas de mujer. Creo que se estaba volviendo esto una bola de maricones y cuarenta y unos y pensaron con acierto que el Ejército siempre es el Ejército, esté como esté, y que era mejor que tuvieran entrada libre las *pizcapochas*. (470)

> [In the past, they say, no woman was allowed to enter here. They used to put camphor in the food and I don't know what else to prevent men from desiring women. I think this was becoming a crowd of faggots and "forty-ones." Then they thought correctly that the army was the army; whatever it is, and that it was better that the prostitutes come over here freely.]

The explicit fear is that the army might lose its virility and become "a crowd of faggots and 'forty-ones' " (a number that has been an emblematic reference to homosexuals since the scandal of the ball of transvestite in 1901, mentioned above.) These precautions that the army was obliged to take imply that effeminacy was possible and that it was considered to be catastrophic to a virile institution such as the army. "The army is the army" is a tautological statement meaning that under no circumstance should effeminacy be permitted to weaken soldiers, as virility is intrinsic to the army. This corollary allows us to argue that constant reiteration and reinforcement of heterosexuality can construct national virility. The reiteration presupposes a necessary hygiene as a prophylactic precaution to maintain national strength. The state institutions that are in charge of controlling bodies equate maintenance of the virility of the army with maintenance of the nation's health.

As we observe in the literary instances included in this chapter, homosociety can be defined as a veneration of the male body, although constrained by homophobic law. Homophobia, on the other hand, is characterized in terms of fear of effeminacy. Thus in the patriarchal system that dominates Mexican public life, weakness and mannerisms, rather than male-to-male attraction, are considered a social disease. However, the presence of effeminate or virility-deficient characters in the novels of the revolution, as well as in the public sphere, contradicts the norms of virility to such an extent that, as a result of the extrapolation of maleness and its criticism in the intellectual controversies about national cultural activity in the 1920s and 1930s, Mexican intellectuals are inclined to criticize machismo in the national culture, as we will see in the chapters that follow.

5

The Sentimental Men: Educating Machos in Mexican Cinema

In this chapter I examine the construction of masculinity and of the nation in Mexican cinema between the 1930s and the 1950s by addressing the following questions: How is masculinity prescribed as part of the state project in this widely diffused art? What are the characteristics of macho behavior promoted by this cinema? And how do misogyny, homophobia and homosociety function in the construction of hegemonic virility?

As in literature, Mexican classical cinema proposes homosociety as a structure of masculine formation. We can observe this structure in films about the revolution as well as in the *comedia ranchera* [rancher comedy], a melodramatic genre in which machista values are exalted in a festive environment marked by a conservative nostalgia for Porfirian rural life. In this macho melodrama, female characters tend to play two different types of roles. They can serve to enforce some type of moral code or they can be depicted as objects of desire who feel guilty for their own attractiveness. In this way, fear and guilt become two main contributors to misogyny in Mexican cinema. Homophobia is also analyzed as a limit of the homosocial structure in urban films of the 1950s. As with the revolutionary novel, the analysis of these films addresses homoerotic suggestion within machista statements as one of the main paradoxes of the representation of masculinity in Mexican cinema.

Revolutionary Aesthetics and the Featuring of Maleness

After the revolution, the political effort to consolidate the Mexican state spawned diverse types of artistic expression that aimed to define the characteristics of the nation. According to Carlos Bonfil and Carlos Monsiváis (22–26), starting from the 1930s, Mexican cinema took charge of disseminating prototypes that norm collective behaviors and ideas. Indeed, the complex machinery and spectacular resonance of the national film industry made possible the symbolic materials that constituted national gender identities. Melodrama structured this gendered nationality. In the same way that Doris Sommers, in her *Foundational Fictions: The National Romances of Latin America* (30), analyzes the nineteenth-century Spanish American allegory of love narratives to understand the formation of national identities, this chapter explores the allegorical relationship between national identity and depictions of masculinity in the classic Mexican cinema—from the 1930s through the 1950s—including the period named "The Golden Age of Mexican Cinema" (the 1940s). As we have stated throughout this book, the formation of a national identity is intrinsic to the formation of masculinity in the Mexican postrevolutionary culture.[1]

During the Lázaro Cárdenas regime, the Department of Filmic Activities was created under the direction of composer Carlos Chávez. Besides short educational materials, this office produced the film *Redes* (directed by Emilio Gómez Muriel and Fred Zinnemann, 1934), which utilized propaganda to foster the collective values that were supposed to consolidate the revolutionary project. Along with artists and intellectuals who defended the idea of a virile nation during the controversies of 1925 and 1932, referred to in chapter 4, Mexican national cinema became a powerful institution concerned with configuring a male-centered culture. *Redes* utilized images of the revolutionary and of the nation's workforce as models of citizenship. Socialist aesthetics are plainly evident in this film, as they are in Mexican muralism. This aesthetic system supported the fissure opened between the church and the state as a result of the *Cristero* conflict (1927–1929).

Sergei M. Eisenstein, the legendary Soviet cinematographer, arrived in Mexico in 1932 to work on ¡Viva México!, a project that was never completed yet had an great impact on subsequent Mexican productions. Eisenstein translated muralist iconography into filmic language. The vast landscapes and the representation of the national collectivity that we find in his work influenced national film aesthetics for decades. In the 1930s, two important factors made cinema propitious for the postrevolutionary project: the masses were already attached to the screen, thanks to the seduction of American, Italian, and German productions, and the soundtrack was a brand-new feature that offered excellent opportunities for ideological dissemination. In 1936, President Lázaro Cárdenas founded the First National Film Archive and decreed that all movie houses must release one Mexican movie per month (Viñas 95). It became evident that the revolutionary state, inclined to control its economy and education, considered cinema a means of citizenship formation. Thus, Mexican cinema became an instrument of indoctrination for the state and a spectacle for the masses.

In the literature and cinema of the postrevolutionary period, representations of men form the core of the discourse that constructs the national imaginary. The thematic axis of this imagery is based on the idea that virility is grounded in homosociety. This is a gregarious world and a highly systematic structure that proposes a society organized to promote history as a male-centered narrative. In this sense, to create the nation is to propose a mythology that renders symbolic the substance of the fatherland, that is, it installs the hegemony of the patriarchy. Here, we understand hegemony as a series of strategies of domination articulated in narrations, images, and concepts that form a coherent whole. It operates through the confluence of power, which universalizes particulars (Butler; Laclau; Zizek 46). Homosocial discourse is legitimated as hegemony when it introduces itself as the means to emancipate the collectivity. Therefore, virility gains consensus as the revolutionary emancipator and thus, becomes the builder of the nation.

Revolutionary aesthetics strive to exalt collective sagas in a metonymy that extends a particular hero's achievements to the society. Hence, this collectivity is concentrated into a homogeneous entity with an unquestionable virility, free of weakness or of feminine mannerisms. Such is the morality of patriotic grounds. Collectivization, besides promoting a socialist ethic, reinforces patriarchal domination. In the films of Emilio Indio Fernández, collective sufferings find relief in the protection of paternal and/or heroic figures: the priest in *María Canderia* (1943), or President Lázaro Cárdernas in *Río escondido* (1947), for instance. In the latter, the vocation of a protective state is allegorized in the paternal figure of the president and shows the patriarchal nature of the national project. In other works of Indio Fernández such as his opera prima *La Isla de la Pasión* (1941), *Flor silvestre* (1943), *Bugambilia* (1944), and *Enamorada* (1946) the plots force fathers to confront their children about the selection of a suitable partner.

Social contrasts involving sentimental narratives are also the recurring themes in these operas. In *La Isla de la Pasión* and *Bugambilia*, poor young men in love with the daughters of powerful oligarchs defend their love to the death. In *Flor Silvestre*, the son of a hacienda owner, José Luis, becomes a revolutionary who secretly marries Esperanza, a poor peasant girl. After an attack by a group of bandits pretending to be revolutionaries (a motif we can also find in Fernández's film *Las abandonadas*), José Luis dies trying to rescue Esperanza and their young son. In this sense, young male lovers opposed to powerful fathers are also depicted as heroes for the collectivity. The romance of the new Mexican state is then proposed as a nascent melodramatic generation in which fighting for love and fighting for justice concur. Masculine characters form amorous relationships that cross social boundaries and often confront the powerful men of the old hegemonic generation. The young heroes do not necessarily succeed. Instead, sacrifice and frustration turn romances into an inexorable pathos evident in much postrevolutionary art. As we observed in chapter 4, revolutionary novels tend to present the revolution in terms of senseless destruction. Among painters, José Clemente Orozco's and David Alfaro Siqueiros' works is worth mention. These lead to a pessimistic interpretation of social reality that contrasts sharply with the optimism of socialist art.[2] The hero in the romances of Indio Fernández, mostly interpreted by Pedro Armendáriz, does not represent a revolutionary, but rather a defeated project that can be explained at least in two aspects: (a) it does not alter the patriarchy as the fight between the young hero and the old oligarch only establishes a continuity in male supremacy; (b) and it does not propose a revolution in terms of social transformation. Instead, it seems to establish a fatalist statement about the immobility of the national oligarchy.

Masculine Melodrama or the Configuration of Machismo and Misogyny

Rather than revolutionary optimism, it is the constantly painful Mexican history that visibly unfolds in literature, art, and cinema, showing the persistence of the Porfirian culture. Nowhere is the revolution celebrated. Instead, a nostalgic view dominates the cultural panorama. The pathos of the frustrated revolution we mentioned earlier reveals the ineffectiveness of cultural and social transformation proposed by the new state. The nation is basically defined under the same premises of the Porfirian regime. Carlos Monsiváis and Elsa Muñiz concur in their views when they point out the continuity between the values of the Porfirio Díaz era and postrevolutionary Mexico. For Monsiváis,

> Mariano Azuela, Martín Luis Guzmán y José Vascocelos (como después Jorge Cuesta y Salvador Novo) extraen las fundamentaciones éticas de sus diatribas del sistema cultural que los formó, el porfiriato, con su nacionalismo como esperanza de otra nacionalidad, sus mezclas de positivismo y catolicidad y su amor siamés a la dictadura y el progreso. (1977, 27)

> [The ethical assumptions of the diatribes by Mariano Azuela, Martín Luis Guzmán and José Vasconcelos (and later Jorge Cuesta and Salvador Novo) stem from the Porfirian cultural system that educated them, with its nationalism as a hope of another nationality, its mixtures of positivism and Catholicism, and its dual affection for dictatorship and progress.]

The four authors that Monsiváis refers to are the main ideologists of postrevolutionary culture. It is not difficult to notice that motifs of catholic and positivist principles prevail in the postrevolution society. Elsa Muñiz observes that Father Ripalta's Catechism and the *Handbook of Courtesy and Good Manners* by Carreño had purveyed moral education to the middle class from the nineteenth century to the postrevolutionary period (27–28). According to Muñiz's interviews with women who lived during the postrevolutionary period, families that were wealthy in the Porfiriato became middle class in Mexico City. Though the revolution defeated them, the ideological hegemony established during the Porfiriato still dominated Mexican life. The culture of the postrevolutionary period, especially a mass culture such as cinema, supported post-Porfirian conservatism. In Monsiváis' view, images of machismo and of family values constructed the "sentimental greatness" of filmic melodrama in the 1930s (1977, 30–31). Classic Mexican cinema shows us how prudery and honesty were instilled as the traditional moral precepts that founded the Porfirian nation and family. The concept of masculinity shifted from being a product of the challenging delirium of the deadly passions of revolutionary heroes to a subdued moral conscience mostly prescribed by maternal voices. Part of this shift included the rise of the filmic genre, *comedia ranchera* [Country Comedy], which featured singing *charros* [Mexican cowboys] who lived on haciendas—large ranching estates of the Porfirian era—and who consistently fought over women or gambling debts, or sought to avenge some familial wrongdoing.

The image of masculinity depicted by the *comedia ranchera* is not one of an emancipatory hero as in the revolutionary novel or even in Emilio Indio Fernández's films. It is that of a hero detached from historical necessity. The *comedia ranchera* depicts a heroic figure without heroic actions—forceful, bellicose men who lack the ability and inclination to fight against oppression. The social structure of *Allá en el Rancho Grande* (1936) and *Los tres García* (1946)—two paradigmatic instances of this genre—evoke an idealized feudal society located within the prerevolutionary hacienda system, despite the process of agrarian reform that had already begun at the time these pictures were produced. While in the revolutionary novel, an admiration for virility goes hand in hand with brave actions taken on behalf of the collectivity, in the *comedia ranchera*, melodrama invents a sentimentalized macho supremacy and the audience is educated in the virtues of violence, much to the lament of the macho characters.

Los tres García by Ismael Rodríguez is probably the most eloquent film to describe the contradictions that characterize the macho: outburst and moral contention, rebelliousness and subjection. In this film, the grandmother, Luisa García (Sara García) represents the feminine saintliness that stifles most of the absurd whims of the male characters. Outburst and contention, rebelliousness and subjection are the movements of systole and diastole of the machista society's emotional and moral economy as represented in popular Mexican cinema.

Luisa García is a widow who owns an estate; her children have been killed as a result of a chain of vengeance that her family has perpetuated with the López family for generations. Her three grandchildren are expected to continue this rivalry, to use weapons, to seduce women, and to pay unconditional obedience to their grandmother's will, even when the law states otherwise. Each of the grandchildren is stereotypically characterized: Luis Antonio (Pedro Infante) is a ladies' man who sings and seduces all the women in town; José Luis (Abel Salazar) is a resentful, sentimental, and proud man; and Luis Manuel (Víctor Manuel Mendoza) is a successful and arrogant professional. The grandmother does not reprimand their vices or defects, nor their cowardice or their disrespect for her. She encourages them to fight, as she tells the priest when he suggests disarming them: "Prefiero verlos muertos defendiéndose como los hombres a vivos y cobardes" [I prefer to see them killed while defending themselves as men than to see them as live cowards]. Pride, sentimentalism, seduction, revenge, competition, are the principles that define the three García's actions. All this comedy does not seem to critique machismo but stages it as the admired model. It can be associated with the propaganda of virility as an attribute of national culture we discussed in chapter 4. That is the propaganda that conflates being macho and being national and supports the politics of patriarchal hegemony.

In *Los tres Gracía*, the male characters are powerful and desirable. This power is deployed in the constant justification of their use of weapons and it reinforces their bellicose behavior. While their power does not connote political resistance as it does in the characters constructed by Indio Fernández, it does serve to maintain the character's oppressive social position. This violent behavior is combined with a seductive domination which can bee seen in the sequence of dreams where Luis Antonio is kissing Lupita (Marga López), his American cousin whom all three Garcías court throughout the film. A group of women dressed in black appear, crying to get his attention. He tells Lupita that those women are "the abandoned ones," meaning that he abandoned them.[3] The camera focuses on Luis Antonio who gestures disdainfully while the group of women pleads with him. As in the novel of the revolution, the hero's image is placed at the center of the stage as a subject who suffers, seduces, angers, commands, states his opinions, expresses his euphoria or, as in this sequence, poses himself as the unattainable object of desire. His seductiveness is never reprimanded, but always celebrated. At his grandmother's birthday party, he sings, "Dicen que soy mujeriego, no lo puedo remediar" [They say I am a ladies' man, I cannot help it]. If deceiving women and still being desired by them is unavoidable, then machismo must be a natural component of being male, a blessing that Mexican men posses congenitally. The grandmother is there to control, encourage, and to guarantee that traditional machismo is situated at the core of the national identity.

The men display such a wide range of emotions that male sensibility clearly dominates the sentimental education in this film. The man's role as the protagonist is represented as the enunciation and performance of male emotions. His dominion is based on sentimental reasons. Subjectivity only exists by means of discourse; that is, the subject is the simultaneous producer and product of the discourse (Hans 1995, 2). Because it is centered on expressing or displaying emotions, masculinity in Mexican cinema can be described as a subjectivity of emotional exacerbation. The male character expresses his feelings through diatribes, screams, and tears. With those manifestations he establishes his power.

In the film *Coqueta* [Coquettish] (directed by Fernando A. Rivero, 1949) Ramón (Agustín Lara) is a blind cabaret pianist. He takes home a dancer, Marta (Ninón Sevilla), one night after she has drunk too much and fought with other dancers in a rumba contest. The story is reminiscent in many aspects of the novel by Federico Gamboa and the film *Santa* (directed by Antonio Moreno, 1932) that have been paradigmatic for the Mexican film tradition about prostitution. In *Coqueta*, the pianist mistakes the dancer's gestures of gratitude and believes that she is responding to his courting. Actually, she is in love with his son. This produces a rivalry between the two males. In a key sequence, Ramón sings sadly about the dancer's cruelty toward him, while she is listening to him behind the scenes. In the subsequent sequence, Ramon shoots Marta in her dressing room; she dies hours later in the hospital. Starting with the title, the film blames the woman for her fate, while it justifies the pianist's crime, as he expresses his pain as the victimized macho. Here patriarchal morality punishes the woman because her body is desired by a man yet she refuses to be his sexual object (Lagarde 544).

Despite his conflict with these feminine figures (the ones who impose the moral contention—the maternal figure in *Los tres García*—and the one who provokes him to punish her and commit a crime—the desired women in *Coqueta*), the masculine subject finds shelter in the space of homosociety. There, he will find the space of his subjective exaltation and there he will find the perfect backdrop for his performance of the discourses that elevate him to the dominant subject position. However, in Mexican cinema both the man's condemnation by the maternal figure and the sinful woman's condemnation by the man constrain homosociety. Whereas in the novel of the revolution, homosociety depended on heroic circumstance, rationalized in the context of a national emergency, in the classic cinema (which is produced in the same period as the novel of the revolution) moral structures erect a misogynist fence: the blaming mother and the blamed woman are then the two shadows that erode the hedonist sovereignty of the macho. If the macho finds in the homosocial relationship an environment that relieves him of the burden of women's morality, it does not mean that women are completely excluded from homosocial spaces. In homosocial hedonism, the presence of and allusion to women recuperate them as objects of possession and exchange, as Gayle Rubin points out (111).

How then can we characterize masculine homosociety in the classic Mexican cinema? Competition is an obvious answer, as contests of power show the content of men's relationships. *Allá en el Rancho Grande* [Over there in the Big Ranch] (directed by

Fernando de Fuentes, 1936) is based on this competitive logic. José Francisco is an orphan who grew up in Rancho Grande and became the best friend of the master's son, Felipe. José Francisco is secretly in love with Crucita, his stepsister, and has promised to marry her if he wins a horse race in Rancho Chico. Felipe is also attracted to Crucita and pays her stepmother to arrange a date without Crucita's approval. Two servants in the hacienda see Crucita and Felipe walking in the night. José Francisco wins the race and announces his decision to marry Crucita in the cantina. The celebration transforms into an uncomfortable silence as harsh words are exchanged. José Francisco challenges one of the men who said he knew about Crucita's reputation to improvise verses in which he had to prove his accusation. The dialogue in folksongs is a paradigmatic instance of this sort of jousting occurring typically during leisure time. When he arrives at the cantina, a strange atmosphere discourages the celebration. While singing, he realizes that Felipe, the master, and Crucita were secretly and intimately together the previous night. The celebration turns into a dispute about possession, honor, betrayal, and guilt. Men have to prove their moral and physical force to their fellow men in the public space. At the cantina, they disclose private issues, which rather than being considered family concerns, are used to increase or reduce macho prestige in this collectivity. The public space is not used to dispute social issues, such as peasants' exploitation or social welfare, but to discuss private and intimate sentimental matters. In *Allá en el Rancho Grande*, patriarchal moral affairs replace socialist aesthetics as the core of social life. While the aesthetics of *Redes*, and most of the movies directed by Emilio Fernández, give prominence to class struggle, social abuses, and marginalization as national problems, the *comedia ranchera*, of which *Allá en el Rancho Grande* and *Los Tres García* are the most famous instances, ignores these social issues. Rather than a social saga where the hero embodies the national struggle, the *Comedia Ranchera* presents us with a conservative vision of middle-class masculinity. This nostalgia for the Porfirian era suggests a deception about the revolutionary state as well as the emergence of a new urban middle class needing conservative values and national narratives that were innocuous for this conservative view.

Instead of dismissing these foundational works of masculine melodrama in the *comedia ranchera*, we have to acknowledge the fact that even though these films propose a nostalgic prerevolutionary male image, they are completely complicit with the notion of virility that the intellectuals of the revolution defended. In *Allá en el Rancho Grande* and *Los tres García* the foregrounded presence of the masculine body is conceived as the emblem of the nation, as the image is the privileged figure for what is good and desirable for the masses.

As in the novel of the revolution, macho supremacy requires that a system of homosocial values prevail. This system is carried out thanks to the development of performative skills, meaning the execution of actions and the observance of precepts that convey the idea of the macho. According to Judith Butler, gender is constructed through a performative reiteration, which eventually naturalizes it (1993, 8). In the construction of the macho this reiteration is evident in the quantity of films in which a man is the central figure; his leading role is, in many instances, highly exaggerated. In the construction of the macho, reiteration consists not only of a repetition but also of a proliferation of the masculine presence in all aspects of daily life. In this construction, women exist to satisfy male desires or to be repudiated by them; men organize their life around their relationship with other men; norms are created to benefit male supremacy. The norms of Luisa García in *Los tres García* aim to preserve the virility of her grandsons. The pedestal that exalts the male characters in *Los tres García* has room for only two feet; the competition for this exalted position shows how masculine rivalry sustains the meaning of being macho.

We have to recognize that this supremacy is not always expressed in terms of authoritative domination and challenge. Besides the narrative of rivalry for the narrow pedestal of esteem that organizes the sequences of the homosocial plots, we can observe a hedonism of suffering in the lyrics of popular songs. The masculine victim who sings his pain utters a forceful argument that makes the one who causes his tears guilty, as we can see in the film *Coqueta*. In his lyricism, the crying man's argument triumphs based on poetic effectiveness through which he establishes that he deserves his lost possession. Sadness unquestionably authenticates the melodramatic logic. This lyrical intervention sets the ground for a dialogic process that defines the discourse of the suffering man. He who convinces the audience of his victimization legitimates himself in melodrama, as we have stated earlier. This ploy alters the rigid patriarchal moral system, which is problematized by the argument of pain. By means of this performative displacement from ruling to crying, masculine melodrama contradicts machista principles, deviating the ostentatious use of force toward the softness of sentiment.

Ismael Rodríguez's Films: Machos Who Love Machos

A toda máquina [At Full Tilt] and *¿Qué te ha dado esa mujer?* [What Has That Woman Given to You?] (directed by Ismael Rodríguez, in 1951 and 1952, respectively) narrate the adventures of two friends, Pedro (Pedro Infante) and Luis (Luis Aguilar), whose relationship develops from a rivalry spurred by a contest of motorcycle acrobatics that takes place at the Police Department. When the movie begins, Pedro is an ex-convict beggar who convinces Luis to allow him to stay in his apartment. Pedro is as skilled as Luis in acrobatics; that is why the Police Department hires him as Luis' patrolling partner. In a dialogue with the building's concierge, Luis explains that Pedro had moved into his apartment because Pedro needed affection. The concierge replies, "How is that? Isn't your girlfriend's affection enough?" and Luis answers, "They are very different affections; besides a woman's love, a man needs the affection of a male friend."

As with the grandmother of *Los tres García*, the concierge's intervention on behalf of the heterosexual moral code reminds the audience that Luis should orient his amorous feelings toward his girlfriend. Luis' answer conveys the homosocial norm in which a male friend is part of a man's affective requirements. The terms in question are girlfriend-male friend and love-affection. Throughout both films, the negotiation between these terms will be carefully treated so as to avoid violating either the heterosexual or the homosocial norms. Allusions to homosexual desire are always imminent, but never explicit. The actions of both characters blur the distinctions between categories that define love and friendly relationships, as assumed by social standards. By alternatively expressing aggression and affection, these friends often confuse the differences between romantic love and friendship. After a fight in which Luis throws Pedro out of his apartment, Luis returns home from work and finds that Pedro has not yet left. Luis tries to expulse Pedro violently:

> *Luis:* ¿A usted nunca le han roto la boca?
> *Pedro:* ¡Huy! montones de veces.
> *Luis:* ¿Sabe que me están dando muchas ganas de rompérsela?
> *Pedro:* Pues no se las aguante, lo menos que puedo hacer es darle gusto a un amigo . . . Ande rómpamela, ande. (*espera a que Luis lo golpee sin ponerse en guardia.*)
> *Luis:* No, así no: defiéndase.
> *Pedro:* No señor, porque en un descuido podría rompérsela yo a usted y eso me dolería mucho.

> [*Luis:* Has anyone ever broken your jaw?
> *Pedro:* Oh yes, many times.
> *Luis:* You know what? I am ready to break it now.
> *Pedro:* Then do it, the least I could do is please my friend . . . please, go to it. (*Pedro poses to receive a blow.*)
> *Luis:* No, defend yourself.
> *Pedro:* No, sir, because I could break yours too; and that it would hurt me a lot.]

By refusing to fight Luis, Pedro neutralizes the homosocial norm that commands that a challenge to fight be accepted. At first glance, it can be argued that since Pedro needs a place to live, he would do anything to convince Luis to let him stay. Nevertheless, the context of mutual seduction aims to keep the friendship because they need each other's company.

Even though the challenge is neutralized when the friendship is in danger, Luis and Pedro keep up a symmetric competition throughout the two films. They prefer to compete in acrobatics and in seducing women. In a nightclub sequence, Luis attracts the attention of an American woman who is talking to Pedro by singing to her. The latter tries to reclaim her attention with caresses and kisses. Right after that, Pedro sings while Luis sits next to the American woman and repeats his advances. They compete over who is more attractive, and the reaction of women is the measure of success. Women are seen as trophies that the men seek ceaselessly with intrigues and treacheries. Luis and Pedro use women as mediators for their relationship. The plot of the film consists of a chain of traps that each prepares for the other to the point of violence. Because Luis is busy in his adventures with Pedro, he neglects his relationship with Guillermina, his girlfriend. For that reason she breaks off the relationship. Intending to reconcile, Luis invites her to his apartment. Pedro then goes through Luis' phone book and on Luis' behalf, invites all the women who he finds listed there to visit him at the same time as the date with Guillermina. When Guillermina arrives, the other women appear as well; they proceed to beat up Guillermina. When the ladies leave, Pedro enters and asks Luis what had happened, as if he does not know. Luis answers by reproducing the women's fight and hitting Pedro. All this violent comedy allows the audience to see a goal the two friends share: to discourage women from approaching them. Competition and jealousy consolidate the exclusivity of this relationship that even neighbors and coworkers celebrate as an intense friendship, thus legitimating this homosocial intimacy.

In the final take of *A toda máquina*, Luis and Pedro are injured after an accident in a dangerous, public motorcycle competition. While riding in the ambulance they say:

> *Luis:* ¿Sabe qué estoy pensando? Que el odio entre nosotros no era odio.
> *Pedro:* Era amistad.
> *Luis:* Siempre había buscado a un amigo hasta que por fin lo encontré en usted.
> *Pedro:* Pues aquí lo tiene (*se dan la mano*) . . . a ver si no pasa nada.
>
> [*Luis:* Do you know what I am thinking? That hate between us was not really hate.
> *Pedro:* It was friendship.
> *Luis:* I had always looked for a friend, and I finally found you.
> *Pedro:* So shake my hand . . . I hope nothing will happen.]

Intrigue caused by jealousy, competition and rivalry, the efforts to keep each other's attention, and this ending, where Luis and Pedro openly state their affection, are components of a romantic comedy, even though using the term romance would be too much for the public's conservative morality.

In the beginning of *¿Qué te ha dado esa mujer?* a continuation of *A toda máquina*, the relationship between these two characters evades a clear definition. In the first sequence, the building concierge catches Pedro in a romantic conversation with a woman on the phone. Pedro asks her not to tell Luis, because they have a pact to eschew marriage. When Luis arrives, the concierge notes he has lipstick traces on his face. Luis tells her that Pedro must not know that he has a girlfriend. The structure of this film shows the same symmetric pattern as that of *A toda máquina*. This beginning is provocative. The audience, which has already seen the ending of *A toda máquina*, could interpret from the beginning of *¿Qué te ha dado esa mujer?* that, in fact, Pedro and Luis live out a romantic relationship. The following sequence refutes this interpretation, however, by offering other aspects of their pact: they will eschew marriage so that they can share their affairs and live a life of parties and promiscuity. That is, they will privilege the homosocial hedonism that characterizes macho activities in the classic cinema over the "danger" of being tied to familial dynamics, which would prevent them from the joys of men. This joy is not presented as homoerotic but as heterosexual promiscuity. Misogyny reaffirms Luis and Pedro's machismo and keeps them safe from marriage. Both men avoid emotional commitment to women, yet impose themselves upon the women sexually. In homosocial norms the only legitimate affection occurs between men.

The conflict of *¿Qué te ha dado esa mujer?* develops around this homosocial and misogynist agreement. Pedro feels betrayed because Luis is planning to marry his girlfriend Marianela. They constantly exchange reproaches, humiliations, and blackmail, producing phrases whose painful lyricism plunges this film into the tradition of romantic melodrama. The grieving song that Pedro sings because Luis has abandoned him to get married, is the cry of a deceived lover:

¿Qué te ha dado esa mujer que te tiene tan engrido,
querido amigo?
Querido amigo, yo no sé lo que te ha dado.

Cada que la veo venir se agacha se va de lado, querido amigo,
querido amigo más valia mejor morir.
Si el propósito lo hiciera de dejarla . . .
tu destino es comprenderla y olvidarla.

[What has that woman given to you that made you so dependant on her,
my dear friend?
Oh, my dear friend, I don't know what she has given to you.
When I see her coming by, she crouches down and looks away, my dear
friend, my dear friend, it is preferable to die.
If he had the intention of leaving her . . .
Your destiny is to understand her and to forget her.]

This song assumes that falling in love with a woman is a lamentable excess. Then Luis has to forget her by destiny: "Your destiny is to understand her and to forget her." In this song, Pedro suffers as a result of Luis' relationship with Marianela.

Thus, when Pedro suggests Luis' lack of affection, the latter answers:

Luis: Cuidado con lo que dices, ella es lo que más vale para mí.
Pedro: ¿Ella es lo que más vale para ti? ¡Ni hablar!

[*Luis:* Be careful of what you say, she is the most valuable person for
me.
Pedro: So, is she the most valuable person for you? No comment!]

Pedro's answer shows his disappointment. Luis has replaced him with a woman as his first priority. After this falling out, Luis talks ceaselessly about Pedro to Marianela with the result that she falls in love with Pedro based on Luis' admiration for him and she leaves Luis. As Marianela tells Pedro in a sequence where both share grief for Luis' disappointment: "él tiene la culpa, a todas horas me hablaba de usted, de sus gustos, sus penas, sus sueños, sus canciones" [It is his fault; he talked about you all the time, about your tastes, your pains, your dreams, your songs]. The film ends when Luis tries to reconcile with Pedro, offering his hand. Pedro responds with a punch. Luis insists twice, but Pedro hits him again. The coworkers who are present encourage reconciliation until Pedro finally accepts and the relationship is reestablished.

The very close affective relationship between Luis and Pedro is possible, thanks to a chain of challenges that keeps the logic of rivalry functioning as a moral frame of homosociety. Despite their commitment to not get married, the heterosexuality of these characters is never questioned. Because of their competitiveness and their perpetual readiness to respond to challenges, their virility is beyond question. This fact confirms the performative character of gender: being a macho consists of acting macho, even if heterosexual duties are not foresworn.

Between Seduction and Challenge

The system of honor that places one macho face-to-face with another differentiates his enemies from his rivals. Each macho character aims to defeat his rival. The rhetorical forms that structure the moments of rivalry lead us to conceive of political discourse through a machista filter. In *La Cucaracha* [The Cockroach] (directed by Ismael Rodríguez, 1958), the signifying structure of challenge and competition organizes the political motives present in the film. Colonel Zeta (Emilio Fernández) arrives in a town to replace another colonel who had failed to obey an order to send ammunitions to the battle of El Sabino, where Zeta was defeated. His actions follow military protocol until La Cucaracha (María Félix), a woman who functions as lieutenant in the task force in the town, proposes that he become her intimate partner. Colonel Zeta responds as if his honor were in question; therefore, the seduction by La Cucaracha precipitates a sort of duel. La Cucaracha is a masculinized woman: she dresses like a soldier, she is part of the ruling elite of the revolutionary army, and she participates in the homosocial gathering in the cantina. When Colonel Zeta finally visits La Cucaracha in her room, she rejects the flowers and other presents he offers her; in addition, she hits him. "Never hit a man," he says, while subduing her. And then he commands, "Get naked: now you are going to be a woman!"

The following day we see Colonel Zeta and La Cucaracha walking the streets as a couple. She is dressed like woman, her maleness has been dominated and her manner of speaking implies that she is in love. La Cucaracha's masculine dress and her virile behavior attracted Colonel Zeta, who is considered the most macho man of Villa's revolution. She had to be womanized to be his lover. The evolution from masculine to feminine has to be analyzed in the dynamic of challenge that belongs not to the discourse of courtship but to homosocial masculine protocol. La Cucaracha can be considered a macho challenging another macho not to fight but to love. The reversal inserts codes of male honor into the code of romance. In this juxtaposition of codes not only La Cucaracha's performance of maleness is visible but also maleness itself, as performance. This is highlighted again when Colonel Valentín Razo (Pedro Armendáriz), a former lover of La Cucaracha, comes to town to prove he is more macho than Zeta. The latter kills Razo in a duel. If being male is something that has to be proved to be identified, we can summarize all narratives about machos in terms of performance, which is excessive when their actions lead them to the point of death. Hence, performance is not just a game of appearances, but a desperate enactment of identity. Death is preferable to being considered a coward. Even at death, Colonel Razo does not lose his masculine prestige because he dies for being a man. Significantly, *La Cucaracha*'s script includes numerous mentions of death: we came here to die, a good revolutionary dies, his age is enough to die, and so on.

Seduction and challenge are the dramatic motifs of the conflicts that construct macho character. *La Cucaracha* and *Un lugar sin límites* [A Place without Limits] (directed by Arturo Ripstein, 1977)[4] are two films that illustrate these notions. In *La Cucaracha* the challenged man (Colonel Zeta) submits to the criteria of the challenger (La Cucaracha), who puts into play the disjunction of domination or defeat. In *Un lugar sin límites*, La Manuela (Roberto Cobos), a transvestite, seduces Pancho (Gonzalo Vega) with her coy evasion and her seductive dance that provokes him to kiss her. Pancho's friend disapproves of the kiss, which explodes into the final sequence in which Pancho pursues Manuela and kills her. La Cucaracha's challenge reinstitutes the heterosexual norm: a masculine woman challenges the macho to feminize her. In *Un lugar sin límites* La Manuela is punished for breaking the heterosexual norm: the effeminate character makes the macho expose his homoerotic desire, which puts his virility into question and thus unleashes the homophobic fury. In this case, to seduce does not mean to impose rules, as in the challenge, but to escape norms. Challenge and seduction, as we can observe in these cases, reveal a necessary relationship between masculine melodrama and patriarchal morals: women should not act like men and men should not be effeminate. Challenge reinstitutes femininity but seduction breaks the norm; the feminization of the woman is celebrated while the homosexual seduction ends in punishment.

How challenge and seduction function in the system of desire definitively differentiates them. Challenge is not outside the law, and for that reason it cannot be a term related to seduction, as Baudrillard proposes (7). Seduction endangers gender identities, that is, the social order of desire. La Manuela is seductive precisely because she produces a desire that is not normative and that destabilizes Pancho's identity. If we come back to *A toda máquina* and *¿Qué te ha dado esa mujer?* trying to understand the meaning of challenge and desire, we have to ask whether the challenging relationship between Pedro and Luis implies a seduction that is denied or hidden behind competition. They keep their desire hidden under the logic of rivalry rather than embedded in an erotic seduction, as is the case in *Un lugar sin límites*.

Hence a discourse of the corporeal sanctions rivalry as positive indicator for homosocial relations and condemns eroticism. This distinction between forms of masculine intimacies should be considered a point of departure in the deconstruction of homosociety: rivalry is absent in Manuela's erotic approach to Pancho, and the disclosure of desire explodes into tragedy, while the rivalry between Pedro and Luis keeps desire out of the danger zone of transgression. Following these approaching bodies we enter a liminal zone where desire is either disclosed, hidden, or suggested. Mexican cinema places the construction of male bodies on this threshold of desire and its constraints. A common factor between the seductive and the challenging relationship is the presence of violence, a constant thread in the fabric of masculine representation, which will receive greater attention in the chapters that follow.

Part 3

Enlightening Machismo

6

Building on the Negative:
The Diagnosis of the Nation

This chapter discusses the works *Perfil del hombre y la cultura en México* [The Profile of the Man and the Culture in Mexico] by Samuel Ramos (1934) and *El laberinto de la soledad* [The Labyrinth of Solitude] by Octavio Paz (1950), that are paradigmatic in analyzing machismo in Mexican culture. These works are essential for understanding the critique of machismo as a discourse of modernity and as a condition for constructing the nation in postrevolutionary period. To critique machismo, one must interject upon intellectual discourses (mainly psychoanalysis and philosophical anthropology) as they problematize the relationship between the masculine image and the nation.

The Last Straw of Salvation

Forged in the process of representation that takes place in both public and private spheres, Mexican national history can only be understood in the light of the contradictions we find when analyzing machismo. Now, paraphrasing Hayden White, if national history is nothing but representation (mainly the representation of men), then the task of writing about machismo is the process that produces national contradictions. In postrevolutionary Mexico, essayists such as Samuel Ramos and Octavio Paz created representations of the masculine that overcame polarized controversies about national culture as well as those that celebrated the homosociety we have discussed in the novels of the revolution and the cinematographic productions of the classic cinema, specifically what we have called masculine melodrama. Machismo is one of the central topics of the essays that have analyzed the national identity since the 1930s.

Criticism of machismo emerges at a time when intellectuals sought to quell the barbaric and bloody national myths that the narratives of the revolution had disseminated. That is, to critique machismo is an expression of modernizing the nation. To contextualize this modernization, I must remark on specific historical processes. In the 1930s the *Partido Nacional Revolucionario* (National Revolutionary Party) was created to stop the militarization of the revolutionary government. Eventually, this party will become the *Partido Revolucionario Institucional* [Institutional Revolutionary Party], and will rule the country until 2000. In the 1940s the so-called Mexican Miracle occurred, consisting of economic development mainly propitiated by the irregularities of the international economy during the Second World War. Capitalist development and the beginning of the cold war in the 1950s demanded the reduction of the socialist left, which was expelled from official scene, discarded to an underground or to a circle of compulsive insurgency, continuously defeated by the power of a state fixated on making dissidents disappear.[1]

Critiquing the macho figure transcended the concept of virility associated with revolution and nationality, disputed in the controversies of the 1920s and 1930s mentioned earlier. These controversies led to a reconsideration of nationalism in terms of modernity. To reflect on national identity related to modernity means to speculate critically about ethnicity, gender, and sexuality, in a sort of anthropological and psychoanalytic discourse, as we can see in works by Samuel Ramos and Octavio Paz. Practically all the critical discourses (Marxism, psychoanalysis, feminism, etc.) since this period recognize that machismo is a central problem of the nation. This preoccupation articulates a conceptual constellation where the masculine image appears, as the revolution had proposed, as an allegory of domination, the colonial condition, and the obstacle for modernization.

Critical rationality based on negativity, a discourse inherited from the tradition of dialectical thought, nurtures various essays of this period. For dialectics it is inconceivable to produce knowledge without investigating the contradictions of the object. These works analyze the masculine hegemony to talk about the nation. Masculine hegemony is put into question, not from the feminine view, but from the position of the masculine man of letters who insists on imaging the nation as a male figure. If there is a crisis in the significance of maleness, there is a crisis in the conception of nation as well. Criticism of machismo questions masculine domination, focusing on the factors that support patriarchal rationalization and naturalness. It proposes to derationalize (or denaturalize) the hegemony of the patriarchal nation. Since that time interpreting the masculine negatively has become a procedure to define the nation. Violence and eroticism are the semantic fields in which this criticism evolves.

Reflections about erotic violence lead to a negative conception of the nation. Possessing the other's body implies violence when talking about misogynist and homophobic supremacy. Thus, violent enjoyment entails a destructive element. Reading the literature of the period from Cárdenas to the post-1968 era and focusing on these aspects of masculinity discloses that all the mechanisms of eroticism and its contentions are fundamental for understanding the dynamics of power in Mexico.[2] Pedro Páramo by Juan Rulfo, El laberinto de la soledad by Octavio Paz, Perfil del hombre y la cultura en México by Samuel Ramos, plays and narrative by Elena Garro, essays by Rosario Castellanos, and the narrative and essays by José Revueltas and Carlos Fuentes, among many others, are works in which depiction of the masculine emphasizes guilt, which is the basis of the naturalized dominion of machismo. This posture is designed to contradict narratives of seduction and challenge that we have observed in the popular cinema. They make visible the irrationality of homosociety and heroism.

Is this a criticism of masculine desire? Questioning desire foregrounds the problem of the symbolic order of the nation. The commandment to populate the land, a primary endeavor for nation making, grounded in the heterosexual norm, constitutes the erotic normativity of the nation (Sommer 14–15).[3] Beneath this hegemonic metaphor—that signifies masculine desire as the nation's desire— we can find the way to deconstruct the patriarchal system and its national project when we pay attention to men acting in the world of men, both in homosexual and homosocial spaces. Following R.W. Connell's proposal, according to which gender generates history, we can also say that the consciousness that determines the features of gender also generates the basis for a criticism of the nation. According to Connell, definitions of masculinity are closely linked to the history of institutions and economic structures (Connell 51).

Essays develop knowledge of the masculine subject, his desires, his nauseas, and the tension of his ambiguities. In the exploration of the intimate side of men, writers conceive of the collective imaginary. Critique of machismo is part of the critique of social vices in a sort of psychoanalysis of quotidian behaviors. It is an interpretation of symbols which induce the hidden discourse of the unconscious. In these, the essayists make visible the traces of the "national essence." Hunting the unconscious, these writers develop an archeology of the submerged discourses of social phenomena. Although they seek historical evidence of the symbolic system, their discourses aspire to an essentialist explanation of the national by mythologizing scars and traumas. The mythology of the negative sign conveys the fatality of the bastard nation. The antimoral and antiaesthetic portraits of the national men—such as the peladito of Samuel Ramos, the pachuco of Octavio Paz, the delinquent characters of José Revueltas, and the violent machos of Elena Garro, among other numerous figures—can be considered reiterations of this bastard image.

Repeated representations of the uses and abuses of masculine body depict machismo. As a cultural construction, machismo determines desire, guilt, and rejection. Throughout the twentieth century, machismo detonates cultural criticism in Mexico. From the psychoanalytic speculations of Samuel Ramos to the most recent elaborations of ethnography and cultural studies in gender or queer approaches, the macho figure remains the most intriguing—although the most studied—symbol associated with Mexicanness.[4] We have to emphasize that the question of machismo and national identity are intertwined in the epics of the foundation of the state: Mexican revolutions and the conflicts with United States, for instance, produced heroic masculine images, which inscribe the values of honor and sacrifice for the fatherland (Paredes 17–37). Nevertheless, critics of machismo point to the destructive and irrational domination that originates the majority of social violence. From microcosmic domestic abuse to the misogynist, homosocial, and homophobic hatred, violence is the energy that fuels the machinery of the state.

In his *Perfil del hombre y la cultura en México*, Samuel Ramos' description of males in postrevolutionary Mexico can be considered both a critique of the marginalization of poor urban men and a characterization of powerful men who dominate the public arena of the state. This double gaze leads to an understanding of machismo as a multilayered system that pervades all aspects of the nation. The explanation of individual psychology becomes the explanation of a political system:

> El "pelado" pertenece a una fauna social de categoría ínfima y representa el desecho humano de la gran ciudad. En la jerarquía económica es menos que un proletario y en la intelectual un primitivo. La vida le ha sido hostil por todos lados, y su actitud ante ella es de un negro resentimiento. Es un ser de naturaleza explosiva cuyo trato es peligroso, porque estalla al roce más leve. Sus explosiones son verbales, y tiene como tema la afirmación de sí mismo en un lenguaje grosero y agresivo . . . Es un animal que se entrega a pantomimas de ferocidad para asustar a los demás, haciéndoles creer que es más fuerte y decidor. (Ramos 50)

> [The *pelado* belongs to a tiny category of social fauna that represents the human residue of the big city.[5] In the economic hierarchy he is less than proletarian and in the intellectual one he is a primitive. Life has been hostile to him in every aspect, and his attitude toward it consists of a dark resentment. He is a being of explosive nature and dangerous to approach because he may burst at the most meaningless contact. His explosions are verbal and his topic is self-ostentation which he projects with a rude and an aggressive language . . . He is an animal devoted to pantomimes of ferocity in order to scare others and to make them to believe in his strength and loquaciousness.]

According to Ramos, the "pelado" is an actor immersed in daily life. His acting, that is, imitating an *other* outside himself, does more than compensate for his failures. It is about performing himself, that is, his acting is not a parody of *other* but a performance of his desired self, characterized primarily as aggressive masculinity. In the archives of artistic and intellectual representations of the postrevolutionary culture, this male aggression has been one of the most common topos. This field of representations combines ethnicity (mestizo, Indian, and ladino), psychopathology (the inferiority complex), politics (the colonized man) and sex-gender categories (the naturalization of patriarchal culture). Ramos' book exercises a social psychoanalysis of Mexican men; the result is a psychoanalytic portrait of the nation.

The allegory of the nation is the story of the "pelado": a resented, boastful and loquacious man who comes from the supplementary zone of the social map. Moreover, his characterization belongs to the improvised zone of the revolutionary state. The "pelado" represents the other side of Vasconcelos' cosmic race that combines the best virtues of all races, or the man of the future whom communist muralism mythologized: two propagandistic and utopian images that dominated the construction of national identities after the revolution. In the essays of Samuel Ramos and Octavio Paz (as well as in literary works of José Revueltas, Juan Rulfo, Carlos Fuentes, and others), there is a discussion of the composition of national masculinity embodying a hybrid and bastard type whose narrative is formed solely by unfortunate events. Bad luck and competition incite his actions. We recognize also this explosive combination of bad luck and challenge in a number of films that, as Ramos' essay does, exhibit the contradictions of the mestizo man, whose condition, reduced to a state devoid of privileges and legitimacy, explodes into a compulsive and exalted performance. This is the logic that organizes the characters that Indio Fernández, Pedro Armendáriz, Ignacio López Tarso, and Pedro Infante interpret. They have been dispossessed of love, patrimony, and symbolic goods such as surname and honor. In reaction to this dispossession, they carry out actions that the audience will emotionally legitimate provided that they properly manifest the claims of the dispossessed.

In contrast with this legitimization of the suffering man, observed in cinematic melodrama, the "pelado" (in addition to the pachuco and the lumpen) bears signs of a social pathology. The exalted macho of the revolutionary epic, of the melodrama of the classic cinema, or of the hopeful images proposed by Vasconcelos and the socialist intellectuals are inverted in Ramos' essay; they are resituated at the margin. It is a means of critiquing the revolutionary utopias and hegemonic ideologies. Undoubtedly, Samuel Ramos alludes to controversies of the national culture when he refers to virility as an instrumental value for the "pelado," reducing the emancipating machismo to precariousness: "[El pelado] es como un náufrago que se agita en la nada y descubre de improviso una tabla de salvación: la virilidad" (51) [The pelado is like a shipwrecked sailor who worries in the void of nothingness and discovers suddenly a last straw of salvation: virility]. In the same way that virility is the last resort of a subject who has been reduced to nothingness, nationality comes to alleviate endemic backwardness in relation to the European civilization.

> La reacción nacionalista actual parece, pues, justificada en su resentimiento contra la tendencia cultural europeizante, a la que considera responsable de la desestimación de México por los propios mexicanos. Su hostilidad contra la cultura europea encuentra aún nuevas razones en su favor al considerar los múltiples fracasos ocasionados por el abuso de la imitación extranjera. (21)

> [The current nationalist reaction seems justified by the resentment against the Europeanizing cultural tendency, which is considered the reason why the Mexican himself underestimates Mexico. His hostility against the European culture increases as he considers the multiple failures produced by excessive imitation of foreigners.]

The terms "last straw" or "last resort" for virility and "resentment against the Europeanizing cultural tendency" for nationalism describe a feeling of inferiority that is compensated by the simulation of its opposite: the virile and national supremacy. Hence, nationalism is a consequence of the underestimation of the self. Though it is a countercolonial impulse, the colonizing imitation and the nationalist reaction are both based on the same feeling of inferiority: they are two phases of the same inferiority complex. Thus, Ramos' discourse turns out to be a diagnosis of the national.

If the idea of the nation is itself a product of the modern tradition, because it follows the model of the modern European state, in previously colonized, developing countries such as Mexico, nationalism reacts against the metropolis that produced the notion of nationalism in the first place. This contradiction also influences postcolonial studies, which, according to Neil Lazarus, aim to be the critical apparatus of imperialism based on the theoretical parameters created in the metropolis (9). Ramos points out a similar contradiction in his notion of countercolonial nation. He makes us see this contradictory condition when discussing the incongruity between the constitution of the country and its social reality. This inadequacy results in a climate of illegality:

> [s]i la vida se desenvuelve en dos sentidos distintos, por un lado la ley y por otra la realidad, ésta última será siempre ilegal; y cuando en medio de esta situación abunda el espíritu de rebeldía ciega, dispuesta a estallar con el menor pretexto, nos explicamos la serie interminable de "revoluciones" que hacen de nuestra historia en el XIX un círculo vicioso. (24)

> [If life evolves in two different paths—on the one hand the law and on the other the reality—the latter will always be illegal; then when in the midst of this situation the spirit of blind rebelliousness abounds, ready to explode at the least provocation, we can explain why this unending series of "revolutions" has made our history in the nineteenth century a vicious circle.]

When we cite the disposition of oppressed people to explode easily as the cause of revolution we psychoanalyze history. The state is a result of corporeal convulsions. Ramos finds in the inconstancy of the macho the key to social movements; he reads his diagnosis of the body in historical terms. Following Alfred Adler's perspective, Ramos' psychoanalysis pretends to shed light on the hidden motifs of social desires. In the chapter entitled "Psicoánlisis del mexicano" [Psychoanalysis of the Mexican], Ramos suggests that his psychoanalysis should be understood as a political action, because for a Mexican "es perjudicial ignorar su carácter cuando éste es contrario a su destino" (47) [It is dangerous to ignore his character when it opposes his fate.] To imagine fate opposed to character implies a utopian logic: there is a horizon that the evolution of Mexicanness targets, a sort of providential destiny that has been distracted because of the Mexican's colonized condition. The decolonized state that he yearns for follows the same model of the modern Western state from which it seeks emancipation.

Often, Ramos alludes to exacerbated gestures, which reiteration reveals are simulations, defensively grounded on the colonial resentment. He affirms that the Mexicans' lack of confidence is irrational (54), that nationalism is a compulsive reaction to colonialism (21), and that aggressive machismo is explosive and uncontrollable, and it emerges as a defensive form of self-affirmation (50). These depictions explain the intersection of macho fatalism with the misfortune of the nation. Presentation of the macho's simulative actions as forms of defense, compensation, and relief, interpret social behavior as a syndrome of irrationality.

Postrevolutionary discourses commonly interpret the macho character through the lens of irrationality. From Mariano Azuela, Rodolfo Usigli, and Rubén Romero to Salvador Novo, Octavio Paz, Juan Rulfo and José Revueltas, literary voices attribute the defeats and tribulations of the macho to his feeling of inferiority. In the dense quiet of Revueltas' characters, as well as in the pompous and deceiving loquacity of presidential oratory, and in the comedic cinema of Cantinflas and Tintán, we can observe the construction of an emptied and ambiguous discourse that tends to escape signification. Both the ladino character and the president enact a protocol in their speech that multiplies masks to the point of the undecipherability. The lack of social communication defines a social segregation by the means of hindered meanings, which is evident in the willful mistake, the double entendre, the ellipsis, and the verbosity that proliferate in the performing arts and in political discourses. We have a myriad of examples: the deceptive labyrinths of César in *El gesticulador* [The Gesturer] by Rodolfo Usigli, the oratory strategies of official discourse that Carlos Monsiváis analyzes in *Amor perdido* [Lost Love], the senator who disjoins unions with an incomprehensible discourse in *Las púberes canéforas* [The Adolescent Canephors] by José Joaquín Blanco, among others. Criticism of incomprehensible language is a criticism of authoritarian discourse in many instances. Here, we can perceive that the state intentionally blurs meaning as the distinguishing feature of public language. The description of the macho state as ladino and loquacious is the most reiterated way of criticizing public voices.

In literature, the characterization of the macho also features public humiliation of the other as a way to express supremacy.

Dialogue is a battle of sexual language. While on the one hand, the silence, the blurry verbosity, and the lack of communication are sanctioned social behaviors, on the other, dialogues with sexual content aim to expose the inferiority of the other in a violent sexual communication:

> La terminología del "pelado" abunda en alusiones sexuales que revelan una obsesión fálica, nacida para considerar el órgano sexual como símbolo de la fuerza masculina. En sus combates verbales atribuye al adversario una feminidad imaginaria, reservando para sí el papel masculino. Con este ardid pretende afirmar su superioridad sobre el contrincante. (Ramos 51)

> [The terminology of the "pelado" is nurtured by sexual references that reveal a phallic obsession, which considers that sexual organ the symbol of masculine strength. In his verbal combat, he symbolically emasculates the opponent, reserving for himself the masculine role in order to affirm his superiority.]

The "pelado" is a subject who breaks the norms of verbal prudence in the public space; he is obscene, as he makes visible in public what, according to social norms, should be saved for the private sphere. The macho's unfolding of sexualized arguments aiming to emasculate the other is a homophobic—and misogynist—public manifestation. From here, we can argue, after Foucauldian thought, that homophobia is a public discourse, and therefore a political action that confirms the idea of sexuality as politics.

Top and Bottom: The Position of the Macho

At the core of artistic and intellectual production of the first half of the twentieth century in Mexico, resistance to the macho hegemony finds a way despite the virilizing insistence of some groups such as the "estridentista" poets and the exaltation of masculinity in the cinema. As the expression of machismo is constantly homophobic, it is difficult to detach homoeroticism from macho identity. Men belonging to working, marginalized classes, who can be identified as "pelados" in Samuel Ramos' terms, have established norms for mingling with homosexual men, as we can read in the greater part of so-called gay literature since the 1960s.[7] The public transportation drivers union includes in its bulletin *El Chafirete* texts by Salvador Novo, who was inclined to seduce heterosexual drivers. Sexual encounters between homosexual men of high standing and heterosexual proletarians are referred to in *La estatua de sal* [The Statue of Salt], the autobiography of Novo, and in *Una vida no-velada* [A Nonhidden Life], the biography of Elías Nandino by Enrique Aguilar, among other testimonies. Paradigmatic works such as *El laberinto de la soledad* [The Labyrinth of Solitude] by Octavio Paz, suggest that there is an indissoluble relationship between machismo and homoeroticism. As according to Paz, hermetic and explosive, fearful and rash, simulator and lacking confidence, violent and submissive are the various ambiguities that describe the Mexican macho, he puts into question the monolithic image of the masculine presented in the novels of the revolution, the classical cinema, and muralism. Again and again, *El laberinto de la soledad* extrapolates the relation between the aggressive masculine role and the victimized and passive feminine one. These masculine and feminine roles also develop in the homosocial space of the men-only gathering. The macho is then a macho in relation to another man, whom he must symbolically *chingar* [to rape] or *rajar* [to crack or to chicken out] to keep his macho attributes. In this homosocial space, homosexual references nurture the language of the "albur," a game of words in which the verbal competence means a symbolical rape. The one who wins this verbal fight, gains virile prestige, which implies that machismo cannot be recognized without this sexualized exchange of signs.

Es significativo . . . que el homosexualismo masculino sea considerado con cierta indulgencia, por lo que toca al agente activo. El pasivo, al contrario, es un ser degradado y abyecto. El juego de los "albures"— esto es, el combate verbal hecho de alusiones obscenas y de doble sentido, que tanto se practica en la ciudad de México—transparenta esta ambigua concepción . . . esas palabras están teñidas de alusiones sexualmente agresivas; el perdidoso es poseído, violado, por el otro. Sobre él caen las burlas y escarnios de los espectadores. Así pues, el homosexualismo masculino es tolerado, a condición de que se trate de una violación del agente pasivo. Como en el caso de las relaciones heterosexuales, lo importante es "no abrirse" y, simultáneamente, rajar, herir al contrario. (Paz 2002, 43)

[It is significant that masculine homosexuality is regarded with a certain indulgence, at least in regard to the "top" sexual position. The "bottom" homosexual, on the contrary, is a degraded and abject being. The game of "albures"—that is, the verbal fight with obscene allusions and double meanings, which is a common practice in Mexico City—evidences this ambiguous conception . . . these words are colored by aggressive sexual references; the loser is possessed, raped, by the winner. He suffers taunts and scorn from the spectators. Hence, masculine homosexuality is tolerated, provided it involves the a rape of a passive agent. As in the case of heterosexual relationships, it is important "not to open oneself" but "rajar" or injure the opponent.]

The dividing line between top and bottom (active and passive) homosexuals depends on a verbal game. The macho figure is susceptible to being cracked, opened, or broken. Therefore, we can explain the emergence of homophobia by the constantly imminent threat that the macho will become a passive (bottom) agent. Homophobia, then, has to be understood as the irrational fear of one's own homosexuality, as Boswell observes in a footnote of his book *Homosexuality, Christianity and Tolerance* (46). If as Marina Castañeda points out, virility has to be learned, to be a man requires a series of initiations (25), which leads to the idea that virility is a condition that has to be constantly tested in the "albur." Maleness, then, is a result of a compulsive homophobia that is enacted in homosocial gatherings.

According to Robert M. Irwin, Paz's conception of the relationship between top and bottom homosexuals must be questioned. As Irwin observes, there only exists the male who penetrates and the female who is penetrated, regardless of whether a man or a woman performs this female role. The top-bottom distinction is not so rooted in Mexican culture, as Paz assumed; instead, Irwin points out, there are works such as *Los 41, Novela de crítica social* [The 41, a Novel of Social Criticism] by Eduardo A. Castrejón (1906) that do not mention such a difference (Irwin, 2003 xxiv–xxv). It is important to underscore that the homoerotic practices that Castrejón refers to are contextualized in a social environment different from the ones Paz depicts; therefore Irwin's argument is only valid for the social group he is alluding to, which has encoded homosexual practices as a sentimental relationship between two men attracted to each other, in contrast to the relationship between two men who are torn by the conflicts of homosociety and homophobia. Paz's context coincides with what Eve Sedgwick calls Mediterranean homoeroticism. There, then are, a number of systems of contiguous sexualities that signify homoerotic practices, as further analysis will reveal.

The desirable-desiring image of the masculine body and the homophobia that we have sketched throughout this work are two sides of a singular public presence. They manifest a grounded eroticism that pervades most zones of social life. This system of imagery alerts us to the complex allegory of power relationships that sexual images and discourses represent. As in Freudian psychoanalysis (following the assertions of Michel Foucault in his *History of Sexuality*), the discourse of sexuality becomes, in the works by Samuel Ramos and Octavio Paz, an instrument of social knowledge. Thus, the language of the "pelado," that conveys erotic violence in *El perfil del hombre y la cultura en México*, and the digression on the verb *chingar* in *El laberinto de la soledad*, show this allegorical confluence of masculine domination and violent sexuality. Masculine sex is an instrument for dishonoring, oppressing, and destroying. Power and sexuality are two indissoluble factors in the representation of machismo. By exercising violence, machista sexuality defines hierarchies of sex and gender and carries out two political functions: one, in the field of sexual relationships and the other in the public sphere and in the field of representations of daily life. Violent eroticism manifests in misogyny and homophobia, which have to be depsychologized to be conceived of as power, that is, political issues. By politicizing them, we turn to understanding them as foundations of a system of domination rather than as mere social pathologies. This kind of domination is an exercise of power that operates by scorning the sexual object. It is a dialectic affirmed in negation: a desire that finds its way by not desiring.

To achieve domination, homophobia and masculine desire are integrated into the moral structure of the patriarchy. If according to Victor Siedler patriarchy is a rationality that organizes society at large—that is, a universalization of the particular masculine—homophobia is the element that draws its limits. The relationship between machismo and effeminacy is not precisely oppositional, but dependent as the image of the macho needs effeminacy to constitute itself. Without the abjection of homophobia, machismo is not possible.[8] This leads us to the conclusion that the objective of homophobia is not to eliminate effeminacy but to keep it alive to possess it as an undesirable object to be taken violently. If the theory of desire explains the principles of possession of the object's symbolic value, homophobia reverses this mechanism, regarding the object as symbolically valueless. The object of homophobia is the absence of desire, in the same way Kristeva defines abjection. Then masculine power is generated in a negative politics of desire.

As we have described in the earlier chapters, in the cinema of the first half of the twentieth century, as well as in the novel of the revolution, masculine domination is possible in a homosociety that is structured by the logic of challenge. Let us understand challenge with the terms that Girard uses to explain desire (9–29). There is necessarily a triangle formed by the object and two subjects of desire: the value of the object of desire increases when there is a competition for it. The challenger proposes a competition for the possession of a valuable object; the challenged one confirms that value when he accepts the challenge. Hence, challenge produces desire or at least the actions aimed to demonstrate supremacy. In the representations of violent eroticism of Ramos and Paz, this supremacy entails a constant feminization of other men to ensure domination. In the game of "albur," and other forms of erotic violence, challenge is used to depower or to strip the sparring partner of value.

The other side of this logic of depowering the *other* is the seduction of a macho by another man, that is, turning the macho into an object of desire as we have observed in the film version by Arturo Ripstein of *Un lugar sin límites.* In both the challenge of "albur," that feminizes the rival, and the seduction of the macho by the effeminate, we can observe that the order of masculine homosociety is not subsumed by the binary rules of gender. The system confirms the criticism of gender roles that Connell proposes in his book *Masculinities,* according to which the study of gender relationships cannot depart from a defined and finite structure, provided that its configuration is ubiquitous and contradictory. One of the contradictions we can emphasize in the works of Samuel

Ramos and Octavio Paz is the construction of desire on the basis of non-desire. These movements of desire and rejection intersect continuously and constitute a complex power relationship that is not circumscribed by the masculine circle, but extends into the society as well. This dynamic opens the way for understanding the cultural foundations of social violence.

7

Inferiority and Rancor:
The Fearful Mestizo

In this chapter I focus on three figures: the revolutionary leftist in *Los días terrenales* (1949) by José Revueltas, the president in various texts such as *Amor perdido* (1977) by Carlos Monsiváis and *El ogro filantrópico* (1979) by Octavio Paz, and the intrinsic relationship between homoeroticism and machismo in some plays by Hugo Argüelles. In these works the internal contradictions that make the macho a melancholic and violent character are disclosed. Mexican machismo is rooted in coloniality, which does not mean that it reproduces the European masculinity model, in its rationality and dominance. Rather, the condition of cultural and economic dependency produces a rancorous and insecure character that is readable in the types of political leadership, namely the orthodoxy of leftists and the protective dominance of the presidents. My main objective is to show that coloniality is not a continuity of the Western culture, but a resistance that is expressed in the nationalist patriarchy, in hypocritical morality, and in an undefined sexuality that places machismo beyond heterosexuality.

Enjoying the Truth, José Revueltas and the Patriarchal Left

In his chronicle, "visión del Paricutín" [The Vision of the Paricutín] (1943), José Revueltas reflects, as he is reading the biography of Francisco Pizarro and traveling to Michoacán, on the

Indians' and mestizos' ambiguous attitude toward outsiders. This biography of the Spanish conqueror of the Inca Empire is his point of departure to describe the human landscape of the region of the volcano Paricutín that had then erupted (1943).

> Nuestro recelo de indios y mestizos, ese nuestro complejo de inferiori-
> dad—que tiene variedades tan extrañas, tan contradictorias—todo eso
> humillado que tenemos, proviene de cómo fue hecha la conquista, de
> quiénes vinieron para hacerla y del modo como les fue otorgada a los
> conquistadores la merced de conquistar. (18)

> [Our Indians' and mestizos' distrust, our inferiority complex—that has
> strange and contradictory variants—all our humiliation comes from
> how the conquest was carried out, from who came to do it, and from
> the way the conquerors entitled themselves to conquer.]

And further, he adds: "La historia de la conquista está hecha de numerosas felonías que, forzosamente, debieron influir sobre la contextura psicológica de nuestros pueblos, creándoles todo eso triste, resentido, lleno de desconfianza y prevención que tienen" (18) [The history of the conquest was made of numerous felonies that should definitely influence the psychological texture of our people, creating in them the resentment and reluctance they have].

Revueltas' assertion on the inferiority complex resulting from colonization as a historical root of the resentment of the colonized meets with consensus in the community of the national intelligentsia. Nevertheless, the depiction of the mestizo cannot be reduced to the dark side of rancor, resentment, sadness, insecurity, inscrutability and such similar emotions. We have to underscore that hedonism, explosiveness, and sensuality are prominent aspects of his character-ization too.[1] As Revueltas observes, those same mestizos and Indians from Michoacán confront fatality with drunkenness, in which pain becomes euphoria.

Reflection on the colonial roots of the character of Mexican men is a constant motif in the literature and humanities of the twentieth century. The hybrid and bastard subject is an image that inundates the historical and anthropological speculations which result in a sort of historicized and mythological psychology. Such are the representations of the macho subject. If we take a look at the archives which contain reflections on national identity, we must consider a number of outstanding essays and chronicles: besides Ramos, Paz, and Revueltas, the works by Carlos Monsiváis, Carlos Fuentes, Luis Villoro, José Joaquín Blanco, Emilio Uranga, among others, offer different aspects of this subject, in a mixture of philosophy, anthropology, and political and cultural criticism.

But Mexican intellectuals are not the only ones concerned with explaining Mexican culture and politics in relation to the mestizo and Indian man. Among others, Oscar Lewis, Erick Fromm, Michael Maccoby, and various foreign novelists, treat this topic seriously. Following the preoccupations of Mexican intellectuals with providing a social psychoanalysis, Erick Fromm and Michael Maccoby carried out around 1950 an ethnographic work on the rural communities near Mexico City, entitled *Sociopsicoanálisis del campesino mexicano: Estudio de la economía y la psicología de una comunidad rural* [Social Psychoanalysis of Mexican Peasants: A Study on Economics and Psychology of a Rural Community]. The two authors observe that machismo stems from fear of women, as it compensates for insecurity, weakness, and for dependence on them (223). While rancor toward the destructive paternal figure of the conqueror explains the bastard condition, the characterization of the peasants in Fromm and Maccoby is related to a phobia of women. A macho compensation, the phobia's function is fictitious. The macho develops it in his imagining of his own liberation from fear; the compensation is then derived as a manifestation of the phobia. Thus, the macho seems to build a wall around himself. In Ramos and Paz, as we observed, the "albur" is a verbal aggression that diminishes the other's virility and puts homophobia into effect. In Fromm and Maccoby, the fear of the feminine reveals a fear of devirilization through the guilt and weakness that women impose on men and thereby subdue them.

Hedonism comes as a "last straw," as an alienated position that mitigates the suffering of the inferiority complex. But this compensation does not alleviate the troubles that constitute the macho character. Ramos and Revueltas prescribe consciousness as a way to break the cycle of machismo's inferiority complex. In the same way that Ramos suggests the recognition of machismo as a first step in the nation's therapy, Revueltas contrasts the notions of consciousness and delight to point out the historical ground of the macho's cultural discomfort.

> De una manera gruesa el problema podría plantearse así: la civilización . . . ha sido inventada para luchar contra el sufrimiento. En cambio la *cultura* tiende por sí misma al sufrimiento. La cultura no es "deleite," sino conciencia; la civilización es placer, deleite y todas esas cosas, menos *conciencia*. (Revueltas 1987, 248 [notes of 1945])
>
> [Rudimentarily the problem can be explained in this way: civilization . . . has been invented to fight against suffering. But *culture* leads to suffering. Culture is not "delight" but consciousness. Civilization is pleasure, delight and the like, but consciousness is not.]

By conceiving delight and pleasure as part of civilization and consciousness as its critical contrary, José Revueltas' thought mounts a criticism of the hedonist body. Critical thought, then, is opposite of the hedonism of civilization, which from his socialist perspective he interprets as a capitalist illusion. Departing from Revueltas' insights, we can propose that the hedonism of civilization stems from colonization and modernity, those exogenous and, paradoxically, internalized processes that, as we have argued throughout this work, produce the inferiority complex that defines machismo.

In the critical undertone that the two most controversial Revueltas novels articulate, we can find the contradictions of machismo in the political practice of socialist characters, one of the dominant topics of his narratives. The novel *Los días terrenales* [The Earthly Days] (1953) revealed the authoritative style of leftist politics. Revueltas criticized the intolerance and dogmatism of the Stalinist Mexican left. This criticism produced a polemic that forced Revueltas to take the novel off the market. Finally, due to his differences with the leftists, Revueltas was suspended from the party. The novel narrated the activities of the party such as organizing peasants and spreading propaganda. The main characters, Gregorio and Fidel are confronted for their beliefs about what the Communist Party should be, and about the ethics and priorities of the militant. Gregorio is more flexible with his feelings of respect and his aesthetic preferences, whereas Fidel subsumes all his existence under the cause. He neglects, for instance, his family to such an extent that his daughter dies.

Fidel is the most fanatic member of the clandestine Communist Party; he enjoys the possession of the historical truth, which alienates him from his own concrete reality to the point that he condemns all his own ideas or actions that do not conform to his doctrine. Here, the idea of enjoying the truth allows us to comprehend a thoughtful aspect of masculine culture (in the sense of a suffering consciousness proposed by Revueltas). Slavoj Zizek, departing from the Lacanian concept of desire, proposes that enjoyment cannot be understood without a relationship with the *other*. Enjoyment, for this philosopher, depends on the conflict about possession of valuable objects. The *other* enjoys excessively, and what bothers us is his/her ostentatious display of the enjoyment (Zizek 1994, 203). When we read about the construction of Fidel from this conflicted perspective of enjoyment, we can observe an excessive possession of the symbolic goods of truth and supremacy. Rather than objects whose value is established intrinsically, these goods find their meaning in reference to enjoyment, and they are therefore established in the conflict with others. Fidel possesses a truth in the face of others whose ideological weakness threatens the integrity of that truth. That is the excess that makes all orthodoxies unbearable.

Enjoyment is then related more to the feeling of loss than to that of pleasure. Thus we recuperate the distinction between enjoyment and pleasure that Roland Barthes points out when discussing reading. Similar to Revueltas' distinction between civilization and culture, Barthes' distinction between enjoyment and pleasure highlights the contrast between hedonism and pain. A pleasurable text is comfortable and exciting, while an enjoyable text depends on crisis and a sort of informed anguish (Barthes 25). This coincidence shows a trend of thinking, focused on the conceptual constitution of enjoyment, pleasure, desire, and phobia that goes beyond psychological discourse to intervene in political rationality, precisely the zone where identity conflicts are generated. Thus, enjoyment is the principle that constitutes desire and phobia, two terms that can explain the social psychology of the masculine as well as its supremacy.

To desire is to exercise power over the desired object. In the case of Fidel, there is a desire for supremacy that is legitimated by the possession of the truth. That privilege provides him with a power over others. Therefore his phobia consists of a fear of losing that possession. According to psychoanalyst Charles Odier, phobia is not merely an irrational compulsion, as it is commonly defined, but reason's instrument for the construction of a phobogenous object (75). This reason would be necessarily supremacy. Despite the most tragic misfortunes—the loss of his wife's love and the death of his daughter (Revueltas 1985, 38)—Fidel is loyal to his revolutionary ideology that commands that the historical destiny of an imagined community[2] prevail over difficult circumstances. This clinging to a doctrinal imperative epitomizes a masculine norm and a political behavior which universalize masculine dominion.

This character created by José Revueltas proved the main reason for his expulsion from the Communist Party, even after the author, given his comrades' censorship, decided to stop the novel's circulation. In the controversies with Vicente Lombardo Toledano and Enrique Ramírez y Ramírez, who were part of the executive committee of the Communist Party (Revueltas 1978, 42), Revueltas questions the relationship between ideology and contingency to disqualify the political practice of leftist politicians. This criticism can be applied to patriarchy as well. The abstract universalization of socialism is blind to the specific requirements of love and compassion. This universalism links to a rational enlightenment that, as an instrument of masculine domination, pretends to be the norm for society. If the universal denies the particularly masculine, what really concerns the masculine interest is known as a universal interest. The construction of Fidel as a rational man associated to the macho ethic confirms the terms that Victor Seidler uses to analyze the gender basis of the modern political rationalism of the West:

> Because society has taken as its self-conception since the Enlightenment a version of itself as a "rational" society, and because reason is taken to be the exclusive property of men, this means that the mechanisms of the development of masculinity are in crucial ways the mechanisms of the development of the broader culture. This makes masculinity as power invisible, for the rule of men is simply taken as an expression of reason and "normality." (4)

Criticism of militant orthodoxy becomes criticism of patriarchal rationality. I do not suggest that the description of masculine domination does not include irrationality. As we have seen in a number of instances, the analysis of machismo reveals behaviors, political actions, and representations that are irrational. Fidel's rationality is not precisely opposed to the irrationality of Ramos' "pelado" or Paz's "pachuco"; it is another strategy of masculine hegemony to stand on a pedestal. The criticism applied to Fidel can be understood as a criticism of masculine supremacy, its legitimation, or its justification. According to what Revueltas himself proposed about the distinction between civilization and culture, Fidel is immune to suffering; he walks impassive among life's daily tribulations. His ideal world is opposed to his wife's concrete needs because, being both feminine and ordinary, they are not significant to him. From this we can also interpret this ideological rationality as a detonator for a misogynist phobia.

Pater President and Pater Intelligentsia

On the other side of critical rationality, the irrationality of nationalism nurtures supremacy. In "México una democracia bárbara" [Mexico, a Barbaric Democracy] an essay of political analysis published in 1958 in the context of the election of President Adolfo López Mateos, Revueltas points out the myth of national exceptionalism:

> Existe en el México contemporáneo—digamos el México moderno que nace a una nueva etapa histórica en 1910—una singular propensión, entre muchos de sus hombres más representativos—propensión que a su vez comparte en gran medida el simple ciudadano común—hacia considerar al país y determinadas de sus expresiones como algo único, privativo, que no tiene precedentes de ninguna naturaleza ni analogía respecto a nada que sea ajeno al propio México y a su peculiarísima idiosincracia. (Revueltas 1983, 26)

> [There is in Mexico—in the modern Mexico that starts in 1910—a singular tendency among its most representative men—which is shared by a broad number of common citizens—to consider the country and some of its expressions as something unique, exclusive, without precedents of any sort, nor analogy with respect to anything that is not Mexico and its very peculiar character.]

The absence of a paragon with which to compare, interpret, or rationalize the Mexican, implies that Mexicanness stands beyond reason, even beyond the universalism that outlines the supremacy of the Fidel character in *Los días terrenales*. This ineffable peculiarity of Mexicanness that Revueltas finds in the language of politicians as gestures of nationalist conviction, reiterates the irrationality of nationalism. That is, the national is a means of domination that is irrational and hedonist. Being peculiar is to be unquestionable, self-generated, a sort of theological entity. How strange that we can depart from an inferiority complex and arrive at this apotheosis of irrationality! Is there in the trauma of the mestizo a purification process that leads to this mystification of the national? Undoubtedly, what Revueltas is pointing out is the discourse of authority that commands the happiness of the nation—the sacred party, as Octavio Paz calls the revolution. Happiness closes up the wounds that critical discourse insists on opening. While from the official perspective, the celebration of the nation is an apotheosis, from the viewpoint of negative criticism, it is a disease.

Critical speculation conceives society in terms of excesses. Machismo is then presented as hegemony (meaning a discourse and a political system that pervade as a social consensus), which at the same time must be diminished and extirpated if the nation is to be healed. Besides analyzing the consequences of this critical perspective in the history of the emancipation of those oppressed by patriarchy, we must understand the political conjuncture in which critics present their analysis. In this case we have to address what communicative action is performed by criticism (in a Habermasian sense). The PRI consolidates the most effective totalitarian system of Latin America in the twentieth century; its web controls practically all aspects of society. It asserts this control not only in terms of coercive domination but also as a discursive consensus. The discourse of the president is an emblematic site of the Mexican patriarchy. Therefore criticism of machismo has to be understood as criticism of the totalitarian PRI.

The president talks nonstop to hide the imperfections of the social and economic system; he is tricky and Machiavellian and he deals in complicities throughout a complex web of homosocial relationships, which as we can imagine, engulfs the nation. If the

state mirrors the macho system, then to psychoanalyze men, either
through the cult of death, hedonism, or the trauma of the conquest
has less to do with psychoanalysis itself than with the insistence on
establishing this allegory to enable political criticism.

To talk about the president as the central representative of the
paternalist state implies a system of power grounded on the figure
of the macho. This paternalism is expressed as an authority that
protects subalterns and decides their destiny. Paternalism means
then a responsibility for governing that concentrates on authority
and guarantees that government does not represent but, rather,
protects the masses: domination promotes itself as a generous
gesture that turns out to be an oppressive disempowerment of the
governed. The president is an "inexhaustible dispenser of favors"
as José Hernández Campos says (38). For Octavio Paz the image
of the president is opposed to the *caudillo*, defining the former
with the positive protective attributes of a powerful father, and
the latter with the abusive and cruel image of the military dicta-
tor recurrent in Hispanic political structures (1979, 23). Maybe
the categorization offered by Paz indulges the actual abusive presidential system of the PRI, on the one hand, and does not appreciate the populist basis of the *caudillo*, on the other.

Intellectual discourse reveals an orphan condition in which history's fatal and human problems are mystified, which immobilizes
the subalterns who depend on the goodwill of the patriarch for sur-
vival. Ever since the regime of Miguel Alemán (1940–1946), a
rationality that uses the discourse of modernization and progress
to maintain this patrimonial authority has explained the developing state. This structural and allegorical representation of the president justifies the historic need for patriarchy. As a mechanism for
attaining social well-being, patriarchal rationality rests on the
following bases:

1. A social consensus grounded on so-called common sense that requires
   the figure of the macho as an authority to lead the nation.
2. A homosocial system that entrusts the functioning of politics to complicities and secrets: the famous "tapado," (the covered one) which
   reserves for the president the privilege of naming, at the last moment,
   his successor, and which privileges a select group with the power to
   make major decisions and the license to establish secret pacts.

3. The characterization of the subaltern as incompetent, precarious, dependent, disposable, criminal, and as a body to be punished; in sum, the object of the macho state's corrective and protective actions.
4. The gender basis of political power is a feature of the nation-state.

Political—that is, presidential—machismo is criticized from another paternalist viewpoint, as the critic is also pretending to represent the subaltern. Thus, the authority—let us remember that authority comes from *author*—of Samuel Ramos, Octavio Paz, and José Revueltas is also a patriarchal intervention that proposes itself as the legitimate masculinity. Significantly, these paternalistic configurations generate patriarchal hegemony. Basically, a coercive image of the dominant macho, allegorized in the figure of president, contrasts in a binary with the authoritative/authorial one.[3] To apply José Revueltas' distinction, while the coercive one celebrates the party of *civilization* or hedonism and oppresses at the same time, the authoritative one addresses the crisis (criticism) that the conception of *culture* entails. Nevertheless, neither machismo nor its criticism overcomes paternalism; their opposition to each other is a false conflict because they merge in the same current of masculine supremacy. We have to read the internal contradictions, focusing on enjoyment and pleasure that constitute the subjects of these paternalisms to dismantle the apparatus of macho politics. If according to Spivak, the subject of desire and power is "an irreducible methodological presupposition" (74), it follows that the powerful man is nothing but a theoretically imagined subject who functions as an agent in the representational realm of domination. He is the image of power and desire. Paternalism become more than mere problems of signification when it intervenes in the social reality: it is the source of oppression and violence that power and desire imply.

Homoeroticism as Machismo: Plays of Hugo Argüelles

In discussions of the deconstruction of machismo, the work of Hugo Argüelles deserves particular attention. In his plays, Hugo Argüelles builds a series of symbolic correspondences where homoeroticism, homophobia, and machismo articulate sexual practices and political positions. The central statement that informs his pieces is that homoerotic attraction and rejection play a fundamental role in the construction of Mexican masculinity. By unfolding homoerotic-homophobic contradictions we can recognize that the characterization of the macho conveys an introspective questioning. In this critical introspection, we cannot find a precise "essence" of the masculine but rather its absence. Thus in the constitution of these characters we can observe a process that strips away the macho appearance: his gestures, his makeup, and his dress, until we meet the emptiness. In this sense, machismo, like every gender category—going by Judith Butler—is a performative. This does not mean that the performative aspect is related to a performance art, despite the fact that in this case we are discussing theater. Instead, machismo itself, behind the scenes in social life, is a performed enactment of masculinity. Here, machismo is a game of masks, a quotidian mise-en-scène. In Argüelles' theater we witness the dismounting of that daily-life performance. Gender performance such as machismo consists of a norm exercised reiteratively; it structures the symbolic matrix that establishes the principles that, in turn, construct the coherent bodies. Reflection on this performance in Hugo Argüelles' theater enables us to see in silhouette the artifices that make the patriarchal system possible.

In his family drama, the father-son relationship destabilizes the macho discourse. Following the classic fable, the son who kills his father, the conflict of _Los escarabajos_ [The Beetles] and _Los gallos salvajes_ [The Savage Cocks] offers a reinterpretation of the mestizo bastard proposed by Octavio Paz and the patricide son of _Pedro Páramo_ by Juan Rulfo.

In _Los escarabajos_, Jaime makes himself up in the dressing room with the ashes of his mother in preparation for acting as a transvestite Medea. This play alternates Jaime's monologue with the family conflicts that originate Jaime's identification with his mother. Manichaeism confers a binary structure as well as a melodramatic aspect on this family relationship. His father is crude and oppressive; his mother dies because of her passion for the man who humiliates her. Jaime falls in love with another man in the same way his mother fell for his father. The macho's expression of repugnance and the abject status of the mother and son push them to eliminate their subjectivity. Through a story of excessive cruelty and obstinate submission, this play reveals the constitutive agents of the machista relationship. While in his *Laberinto de la soledad*, Octavio Paz emphasizes the cruelty of the mestizo who *chinga* (violates) as a form of revenge against his bastard condition, Argüelles depicts a bastard whose heroic aspirations are reduced to the mediocrity of a failed actor and his passionate love toward a man who does not reciprocate his love.

As happens in most of Argüelles' plays, we cannot miss noticing the psychoanalytic subtext. Jaime and his mother have constructed themselves as objects of desire that never encounter reciprocity. Coldness and humiliation are necessary conditions for masochist pleasure, as Guiles Deleuze observes (1991, 117). Nevertheless, considering that Jaime and his mother are fictional characters that Argüelles intended to deploy before the theater audience, their psychological features invoke an interpretation that supersedes mere psychic specificity. They are propositions that concern a cultural system of machismo. In these cases, the system of machismo can be imagined as a machine that produces abject subjects. The mother and her homosexual son's subjectivity are articulated in the macho's hateful performance. Talking to the mirror, while he cross-dresses and applies makeup, the mask made with his mother's ashes, Jaime stands at the threshold between the dressing room and the stage, the death and the theater, that is, the interstices of representation.

As a performance, machismo is a representation that is readable in the practice of characterization. In Jaime's incessant arguments with his father, the latter insists on prohibiting his son from telling the truth or expressing passion, the latter of which he considers the vices of degenerates. Jaime had always wanted to be an actor. For his father, theater and homosexuality are evidences of his son's lack of virility. But Jaime decides to become an actor because he wants to experience "algo más intenso y verdadero" (302) [something more intense and real], a confession that is contrary to his father's rule against speaking one's mind. Paradoxically, Jaime sees theater as the space of the real and considers reality a simulation as reality limits the expression of true emotions. The constraints imposed by the father refer to a semiotic structure that can be understood in terms of the contradictory pairs: law-truth, and the imagined reality-the real, that is the law contradicts the truth in the same way that the conceived reality contradicts what is real. The father's word implies a normative objectivity (objective, that is, according to the interests of domination), while passion is a dangerous inner compulsion of the feminine *other* that would open the way to a non-normative realm of the signs or what Teresa de Lauretis locates in the "space off" of the hegemonic discourses (26). The father-son relationship (and its mirror, the father-mother) positions the father against the signs: that is, the father's word constructs a frame that limits the son's language by prohibiting his feminine subjectivity. This relationship brings up the Hegelian master's word that obstructs the slave's verbal intervention and also what Spivak comments about the relationship between mastering Western theory and interdicting the word of the subaltern (74): in both cases, a destabilization of the master's command or of the law, in Hegel, and of theory, in Spivak, enables the dominated subject to speak. On the basis of these premises it is necessary to define the word of the son as a device that dismantles the foundations of the father's domination: the crumbling of Pedro Páramo when his son kills him in the novel by Juan Rulfo works here as a metaphor of the dismantling of patriarchal domination; the macho power falls just at the moment when the word of the son makes it meaningless.

Hugo Argüelles' play *Los gallos salvajes* analyzes, in a quasi-essayist exposition, the father-son relationship in terms that reveal the political contradictions of patriarchy, suggesting an evolution from a macho premodern power to a "civilizing liberation" (337). The son has come back from the city with ideas that are against his father's domination. This scenario confirms that the question of machismo is inseparable from the problem of representation. The father and the son have opposing ideas about masculinity. The father's idea of virility can be summarized in his overvaluation of two actions: killing and copulation. In the insights that the son reveals, machismo is defined from the clinical perspective that names as pathologies what the father considers virtues. At the end of the first act, we discover the tragic background: the two have lived an incestuous relationship since the son was a child.

According to the father, he forced his son to perform fellatio to transmit virile energy to him. For the father, incest is part of macho education: the son will reproduce the father (Judith Butler would say, reiterate him) not only imitating him in his repressive actions as a cacique, but also loving him erotically. Homoeroticism ends up contributing to the formation of the macho, in the father's view. In his critical-clinical discourse, the son defines this relationship as homosexual; the father rejects that term because he does not conceive that theirs is a relationship of *putos* (a pejorative word for homosexuals).

> ¿Pero qué tiene que ver nuestro darnos así, con lo que hacen esos degenerados? ¡No te confundas, Luciano! ¿Qué tiene que ver algo que yo siento puro y noble . . . hasta así; como eso: un rito de comunicarse fuerzas, con . . . ¡No! Te han revuelto la mente! ¡Cuántas veces te dije: "El macho se distingue por su verga, y si ésta le da placer, mientras la meta dentro o quede arriba, no tiene por qué negarse su contento"! ¡Carajo! ¡Cualquier hombre lo sabe! (353)

> [But what has our giving ourselves in this way got to do with what those degenerates do? Don't get confused, Luciano! What it does have to do with is my feeling which is pure and noble . . . like that, a ritual of communicating strength, with . . . No! They have confused your mind! How many times have I told you: "the macho is distinct because of his penis and if the penis provides pleasure to him, whether he puts it in or leaves it out, there is no reason to deny its content!" Damn it! Every man knows that!]

The sexuality that is concentrated in the penis—according to the father—cannot be considered homosexuality, a term that does not belong to his vocabulary but to the Western medical discourse. In this statement macho homoeroticism does not define a sexual attraction for another man, which would imply surrender to the other's penis—thus a feminization and loss of virility—but the enjoyment of one's own: an autoeroticism. The son's criticism resignifies macho discourse as pathology. The father's words are rooted in valuing the symbolic benefit of homoeroticism. This value privileges bisexuality over heterosexuality and homosexuality, but it is a bisexuality that can be understood only in terms of a double standard.[4]

The clash between two universes of representation, namely the macho discourse of a double standard confronting the discourse of pathology that stigmatizes homoeroticism, expresses the central conflict of this tragedy. The guilt produced by the system of pathological representations defining the son as castrated and dyslexic, explodes into a bloody ending. Luciano kills his father. This action reiterates the image of the patricidal son rooted in the characterization of the bastard mestizo that we have observed as a constant topic of Mexican literature. This work adds the homoerotic incest to that tradition, which son and father represent in two different ways; for the father it cannot be homosexuality, for the son it is a stigma that makes him murder his father. This clinical regulation of gender rules and constructs bodies. Social discourse generates masculinity on the basis of the pathology of machismo and homophobia. It is necessary to depathologize these terms, to elevate them from symptoms to representations, and to comprehend the production of the masculine body as the core of the power system. Guilt and the double standard then produce power by constructing masculinity. Therefore, we cannot but interpret this power in terms of violence, the exacerbation of this masculinity.

In *El ritual de la salamandra* [The Salamander's Ritual], Antonio, from a prominent family in the political class, discloses the mechanisms of the double standard as follows:

> La mujer con quien me casen será la típica almohada con hoyo . . . y todas las credenciales en regla: ¡dinero, sitio social, bonita, babosa y decente! ¡Un sueño del establishment! Y a cambio yo seré por los años que viva "un júnior asegurado" . . . Prefiero vivir lo "otro" . . . como hago: de vez en cuando con mis amigos . . . y ya "motos," "pasados" y borrachos . . . todo. Pero al día siguiente ni quien hable de ellos. (219)

> [The woman they choose for me to marry will be the typical pillow with a hole . . . and with all her credentials in order: money, social position, pretty, stupid, and decent! A dream of the establishment! In exchange I will be my whole life "a successful junior" . . . I prefer to live the other way . . . in my way: once in a while with my friends . . . when "high," and drunk . . . all that together. But the next day nobody will talk about it.]

For Antonio the heterosexual male role is inauthentic, though that does not mean that his clandestine sexuality is authentic. In his relentless determination for exposing social norms, Argüelles' work cancels out any possibility of authenticity. On the one hand, homoerotic contacts are enclosed in secrecy; they cannot be named, they end up nonexistent, and reduced to the unmentionable. On the other hand, marital life aims for the observance of social rules. That means it is pure discourse, an emptied sign whose purpose is to guarantee membership in the system of privileges. Between the gestures of social performance and the absence of signs of the fleeting homoeroticism, the subject of the double standard lives in the liminal space. In this space sexuality tends to be designified and the gender category of the heterosexual man tends to be desexualized. Through these fluctuating signs we see the works of Hugo Argüelles dismounting the symbolic structure of patriarchy.

This enterprise of depowering the patriarchy goes to the comedic extreme in *El retablo del gran relajo* [The Sketch of the Great Fun], where the cacique's possession of Napoleon's penis, rather than providing the power and virility that was promised to him, effeminizes him. This farce erodes the monolithic presence of masculine dominion by exposing the vulnerability of the macho and his imminent effeminacy. After virility collapses, though, neither the feminine nor the homosexual takes dominion. What happens is the disarticulation of the gender system. We can deduce from Argüelles' pieces that the masculine does not exist without the mirror of the feminine, its counterimage.

Part 4

Vanishing Identities

8

Mayate: The Queerest Queer

This chapter discusses three novels of the so-called Mexican gay literature from the 1960s through the 1980s: *Después de todo* (1969) [After All] by José Ceballos Maldonado, *El vampiro de la colonia Roma* (1979) [The Vampire of Roma Neighborhood] by Luis Zapata and *Púberes canéforas* (1983) [Adolescent Canephors] by José Joaquín Blanco, as well as *Amor Chacal* (2000) by Juan Carlos Bautista and Víctor Jaramillo, a tourist-ethnographic documentary on coastal homoeroticism. This chapter focuses on the characterization of the "mayate," a character whose resistance to identifying himself as homosexual, despite his homoerotic practices, challenges the concept of identity and therefore constitutes a relevant object of queer analysis.

Wishing to Be Desired: Ceballos Maldonado

In the novel *Después de todo* [After All] by José Ceballos Maldonado (1969), the protagonist Javier Lavalle, a mature homosexual man, tries to fill the emptiness of his boredom, unemployment, and solitude by writing his memoirs in a modest room he rents in the Colonia Roma, a middle-class neighborhood in Mexico City. From this setting he imagines his past in Guanajuato, where he spent his youth. His story unfolds as a constant tension between the invisibility and the exposure of his sexual relationships with other men. Lavalle talks about his seductive strategies such as furtive adventures, always under the threat of discovery. The most outstanding actions in his remembrances—to hide, to denounce, to watch over, to expose, to blackmail, to simulate, and to dissimulate—refer to his meticulous escape from the social gaze. Lavalle develops two daring skills: to seduce men who do not consider themselves homosexuals and to hide from the gaze of those who could condemn him. Lavalle's power can destabilize both the norm that prohibits homoeroticism and the masculine hegemony that presumes itself impenetrable by seduction. He seduces what is considered unseducible, turning upside down the patriarchal rules. Lavalle learns that he can achieve this destabilization by cultivating the art of secrecy. He confirms Annick Prieur's insight that Mexican society tolerates homoerotic encounters, provided they stay invisible, in a homosocial masculine context, and perfectly dissimulated with euphemisms and absolute discretion (188–189).

Critics of this novel have emphasized the self-affirmation of the homosexual middle-class man. The protagonist-narrator characterizes himself as a homosexual, throughout an episodic chain of sexual encounters with men who are ostensibly heterosexual. Lavalle goes back to his childhood to remember his relationships with pederast priests, classmates, and his assistants in the school laboratory where he used to work. According to Mario Muñoz, Javier Lavalle "en el decurso de los acontecimientos evocados va asumiendo sin ninguna culpabilidad su condición homosexual pese a los desagradables contratiempos que esta forma de conciencia le acarrea" (15) [in the development of the remembered events assumes his homosexual condition without guilt, even though this consciousness brings unpleasant setbacks]. Luis Mario Schneider, on his part, observes that Ceballos Maldonado "descubre los mecanismos del cinismo como única posibilidad de autoafirmación para salvarse de los prejuicios que una sociedad intolerante exige a la marginación homosexual" (75) [discovers the mechanisms of cynicism as the only form of self-affirmation to liberate oneself from prejudices that an intolerant society demands from the homosexual marginality]. The self-affirmation Schneider refers to results from associating guilt with seduction, a combination whose roots we can find in the hypermasculine myth of Don Juan, where seduction challenges the role of guilt in the moral system of the Catholic Church. Seduction focuses on men who, despite their participation in male-to-male sexual contacts, reject identifying themselves as homosexuals or bisexuals. This lack of definition characterizes the *mayate, chichifo,* or *chacal,* a subject that is prevalent but invisible in the panorama of Mexican masculinities. These three terms traditionally name the person who plays the penetrating role in homoerotic intercourse, who is characterized further by his reluctance to express attraction toward his sexual partner (Prieur 189).

Mayate, chichifo, and *chacal* are words that belong to the discourses of the *joto* (the man who plays the passive role in homoerotic intercourse; to whom we usually also ascribe feminine characteristics). The *joto* objectifies his "top" partner with these designations and thus the effeminate man claims his subject position and uses the power of representation over his object of desire. In her ethnographic work on transvestites in Mexico City, Prieur finds that these labels are exclusively used in homosexual jargon (189). In general, these three terms are synonyms, although they can be nuanced as follows: *chichifo* connotes prostitution or giving sex for favors; *mayate* describes the top position, not necessarily related to expressed prostitution; and *chacal* is applied to individuals who are uncultured and mostly marginal and from the countryside. These differences are anything but fixed. The word *mayate,* the most common, comes from *mayatl,* a náhuatl word (the language of the Aztecs) for a species of bright green beetle whose larvae grow in manure. *Mayate* then is an allusion to the colorful proletarian man's dress, as well as a fecal metonym to describe his sexuality. *Chacal* comes from *chacatl,* also from náhuatl, which refers to a species of shrimp that has a scorpion form. The ferocious appearance of the *chacal* and its edibility connotes a savage sensuality. On the other hand, the words *joto* and *choto* (whose root seems to be the Gypsy verb *chotear,* to make fun or to mock) define an effeminate man who is socially stigmatized.

The main difference between the *mayate* and the *joto* is the lack of self-definition in the former and the derogatory visibility of the latter. In the presence of those *mayates* who reject identification and expression of desire, the cynicism of Javier Lavalle enables his self-affirmation and produces their desire for him. In the novel, the moments of seduction become a struggle between the lack of desire

and its provocation. For instance, in an episode in which Lavalle
stops bombarding Gastón—one of his seduced *mayates*—with sexual insinuations, he describes how Gastón's desire emerges as follows: "[m]ientras charlamos él ríe, mueve la cabeza, se contonea y
hasta me aprieta el brazo con la mano. Pero sobre todo siento que
me reprocha: 'Eh, tontito, no quisiste. Por fin, ¿eres o no eres?' "
(90–91) [While we chat he laughs, nods his head, swaggers, and
even squeezes my arm. Most important, I feel he reproaches me:
'Hey foolish one, you didn't want, so . . . are you [*joto*] or
not . . .?]. Although Lavalle has produced a desire in Gastón by
suppressing the courtship, their identity situations are the same:
Lavalle has to define himself and Gastón has to remain undefined
to keep the *mayate-joto* relationship intact. Nevertheless, the pre-
tence of being desireless person that Gastón is supposed to keep is
ruined. Possibly being desired by the *mayate* is an invention of
Lavalle's nostalgia that his solitude and poverty foster. The narrative construction of the *mayate*'s desire would then be a strategy of
the narrator's self-affirmation.

In juxtaposition with this nostalgic account, unexpectedly *mayates* erupt in the present tense narration. While Lavalle is writing
his memories, many knock at his window. They are poor young
men, who are not allowed to enter as Lavalle has nothing to give.
They ask for money and offer "lo que usted quiera" [whatever you
want]. These interruptions create fissures in the plot that allow us
to see an aspect of the novel that the narrator hesitates to codify.
Whereas this narrator is meticulous in constructing his own past,
idealizing his sexual encounters and calling them romances, when
talking about the narration in the present, he shows his discomfort
with his visitors. The latter reside on the margins of the story; they
lack citizenship in the narrative of desire that, projected onto the
past, recount what the homosexual would like to be. This lack of
codification lets us see the *mayates'* lack of identity. Lavalle does
not feel desire for these young men, nor they do feel desire for him.
The narrative interest dissolves as the dynamics of seduction are
cancelled. Precisely in these absences of desire we find the most relevant traits of machismo, at least in the field of homoerotic relationships. The disruptive actions, the brief visits and calls from
those men outside the window, function as counterpoints to the

plan of self-affirmation of the homosexual character underlined by Mario Muñoz and Luis Mario Schneider.

Rather than follow the narrative plan of Lavalle's story—clearly oriented to conceive a homosexual identity that departs from resistance against the forces that marginalize him, guilt and macho supremacy—I want to emphasize the liminal position of the *mayate*, whose characterization denies homoerotic desire. Lavalle repeatedly avoids being identified or named as a homosexual, which contrasts with the homosexual identity that Lavalle outlines in his "romances." The episodic structure is periodically interrupted by a *mayate*, establishing a narrative plan based on reiteration. A transversal reading of Lavalle's various romances and the intermittent vignettes of rejected *mayates* opens the way to a discussion of an economy, a morality, and a strategic set of skills of domination that are developed by the individuals involved in homoerotic relationships.

Throughout his life, Lavalle generously gives presents or money to his sexual partners. To give something for intimate contact shows an economy established around the exchange value of sex. This economy implies the existence of a market where pleasure produces a relationship of power where on the one hand, there is power in possessing a valuable piece of goods to offer, and on the other, there is power in the ability to purchase such a piece of goods. While in Lavalle's narrations of the past, he boasts an inexhaustible purchasing power, in the present, with scarce resources to participate in this sexual economy, he has to reject all offers. Thus it seems that Lavalle's sexuality depends on his current financial status. Payment is associated with a lack of desire; therefore, the more the *mayate* resists seduction, the more the *joto* has to pay for sex. This fondness for prostituted contact unmasks the story of the homosexual Don Juan that is revealed in the narration. The financial decline that forces Lavalle into sexual abstinence opens a deep wound in the novel: the protagonist-narrator takes the perspective of someone who is wrecked, having experienced a loss of purchasing power; he has also experienced decline in his capacity for desire. It would seem that the narrative strategy of self-affirmation through seduction is ultimately dependent on his acceptance of economic defeat. The *mayates*, who like Lavalle are unemployed, must look for other windows to knock on to maintain themselves. The characterization of *mayate* as *chichifo* (a prostituted individual, as mentioned earlier) recurs in the literature and in a number of testimonial texts such as memoirs, chronicles, biographies, and ethnographic works.[1] The fact that the *mayate* is a proletarian or an unemployed young man, or somebody who has to choose prostitution as a way of life, positions him as subaltern with respect to the *joto*.

Nevertheless, the dominant position of the *joto* is neutralized if we consider that what he is actually negotiating is his submission to the symbolic domination of the *mayate*. The pact between the *joto* and the *mayate* is based on symbolic and economic value of the virile body; this relationship reinforces and magnifies machismo. The desire for virile domination supports a social dynamic that takes place in the underground community, in a society of enjoyment. There we can observe how a politics and economy of the body is built on the social structure of prestige that defines subjects in the patriarchal system, reflecting the binary relationship masculine-feminine, effeminizing the *joto* and masculinizing the *mayate*. However, that it takes place in the margins problematizes this replica of the patriarchal binary structure. As this gender system is subjected to the multiple simulations that prostitution effects, we can reflect against the grain on the implications of being marginalized.

The condition of marginality defines the *mayate-joto* relationship as emergent. As Nelly Richard states, their identities would claim the "derecho a la singularización de la diferencia contra la represiva uniformidad stándard de la identidad mayoritaria" (12) [the right to singularize their difference against the repressive uniformity of the identity standards of the majority]. However, the *mayate*'s determination to tarry in the zone of the unnamed—and therefore remain invisible—and the *joto*'s feminine strategy of seduction, lead us to realize that this kind of relationship diverges sharply from the identity politics of gay and feminist activism, which seeks liberation from oppression and invisibility. This is due to the *mayate*'s lack of definition as one of his conditions of existence. We have, then, to propose that the *mayate*'s homoeroticism is only possible by escaping signification. In fact, it is significant that in the gay pride marches in Mexico City no sector has represented itself so far as *mayate*, *chichifo*, or *chacal*.

The episodic structure of the novel *Después de todo* makes the *mayate-joto* encounter seem ephemeral and hazardous, which explains their resistance to establishing a clear-cut identity. Since the *mayate* exists only by exception, his self-definition includes nothing about his homoerotic adventure. This undefined sexuality, as well as his resistance to expressing desire toward his male sexual partner reinstalls the *mayate* in a doubtful heterosexuality, although this doubt has more to do with machismo than with heterosexuality per se. The resistance once identified opens the way to an analysis of the subjectivity of *mayate* at the point zero of meaning. As he wanders on the margins of the cartography of sexuality (with respect to identity designations), the *mayate* is always in transit; he never belongs to a fixed category. This contrast between identity and resistance to categorization suggests a distinction between identity and subjectivity. If we accept Jorge Larrain's claim, "la construcción de la identidad es un proceso intersujetivo de reconocimiento mutuo" (46) [the construction of identity is an intersubjective process of mutual recognition], when the *joto* defines the *mayate* as such, by implication he derecognizes his heterosexuality. Yet when the *mayate* defines himself as heterosexual, he recognizes himself within the dominant norm. The obstacle to the recognition of the *mayate* as an identity is the articulation of his desire. Although his sexual practice does not express a desire for the effeminized *joto*'s masculine body, we cannot interpret it as an absence of desire, but only a lack of desire of the *joto*; that is, the *joto*'s body lacks desirability and is not an object for the subject *mayate*. The *joto* is only instrumentalized for the requirements of the *mayate*'s desire but is not his target. Paradoxically, when the *mayate*'s subjectivity denies desire, it finally reveals the structure of his desire. Absence is nothing but presence in the irrevocable certainties of the unconscious. There is the *mayate*-I who objectifies himself as the Other. In the Lacanian mirror, the self-image of the *mayate* is the image of the macho and his body is the body of the macho.His erotic practice, then, consists of wishing to be desired as a virile body. This macho self-image is not a mere simulation but a system of behaviors and a series of meanings that enable the articulation of his subjectivity.

In this deceiving game of mirrors where the *mayate* is the image of the macho and the *joto* a feminine fantasy, what remains is the suspension of homosexual identity along the pendulum of sexualities.

Luis Zapata: The Society of Pleasure

Luis Zapata's *El vampiro de la Colonia Roma* is structured as a transcription of Adonis García's life story. Adonis, living as a prostitute in Mexico City since the death of his mother when he was a teenager, recounts his adventures as a *chichifo* in the manner of a picaresque novel with episodes that show varied social spaces and characters of the city. The novel questions the binary relationship between the masculine and the feminine through a hazardous journey of sexual learning that crosses indifferently through varied erotic practices, superseding traditional homoeroticism. According to Alicia Covarrubias, "[l]a homosexualidad de Adonis explicita ... la intrínseca ambigüedad del pícaro, activo o pasivo, rebelde o servil, conforme le convenga" (187) [the homosexuality of Adonis explains ... the intrinsic ambiguity of the "pícaro," active and passive, rebellious or submissive, depending on his convenience]. Adonis García conceives of his homosexuality as a result of a constant negotiation with his costumers and, in general, with everybody who comes in contact with him. Unlike the *mayate's* invisibility and the double standard in the novel by Ceballos Maldonado, in the novel by Zapata, the openly prostituted presence of the protagonist manifests a subjectivity that escapes all the categories through which he passes. The picaresque structure lets us see a ubiquitous and inconsequent sexuality. Though Adonis García begins his sexual identification as a *chichifo*, he redefines his identity as his body learns new pleasures. The society of pleasure prevents Adonis from settling on an identity, but unlike the *mayates* of Ceballos Maldonado whose deidentification was produced by the absence of desire, in the Zapata character that deidentification is achieved through knowing the others erotically. Despite Adonis' experience with various forms of homoeroticism, he still expresses intolerance for effeminate *jotos*. Adonis lets us see how homophobic hegemony is internalized in the homoerotic relationships (cf. Ortiz

331–332). This hostility toward effeminate homosexuals reiterates the conversion of machismo into homophobia among homosexuals.

The intolerance of effeminacy seems to aim at the derogation of the *mayate-joto* relationship of traditional homoeroticism. When Adonis defines himself as a "homosexual de corazón" [a homosexual at heart] opposed to the more clearly defined binary category, he expresses his resistance to the stigmatization of the *joto* preference for the macho designation. In fact, one of Adonis' most valued characteristics is his virility. The novel's search for a homosexual identity is overcome, according to Mario Muñoz, by an exacerbated eroticism that brings Adonis to self-destruction (16). Similar to macho characters, such as Amado Nervo's Pascual Aguilera or Juan Rulfo's Miguel Páramo, whose virility is interpreted as an imperative eruption of their carnal appetite, the Adonis García's characterization is based on the body overcoming social conventions. The predominance of sensuality as the thematic motif that organizes the narration, which is meant to be read as if it were a transcription of a tape recording, tries to represent itself as a spontaneous testimony to the body's uncontrolled impulses, achieving a parallel between the narration and sexual compulsion. Adonis' dependence on urges that contradict social norms, including the consuetudinary rule of homoerotic relations, define this novel as naturalistic. Thus, Adonis' character seems to be determined by his biological impulses, the inexorable emergence of the psyche that nurtures the Freudian imagination. If the character has fallen complacently into self-destruction, we have to talk about the fatalistic vocation of naturalist characters.

This naturalist interpretation would lead us to blur other utopian propositions the novel suggests. The knowledge and refinement of this character, rather than his decadence, influence our reading. As we noted above, Adonis García knows the others; he is a judge whose episodic experience has brought him through the varied social spaces of Mexico City. This character is an individual in terms of synthesis, that is, he has made an individual consolidation in the *I* of all social desires, as Agnes Heller proposes (115). This social synthesis, readable in a character who has conceived his own body as a device that weaves an extended web of sexual contacts, would establish, then, a community imagined around pleasure or a consensus on the value of pleasure. The space of the bathhouse describes this society of pleasure as a sexual democracy:

> Ahí ves desde señores que dejaron afuera el galaxie y que nomás van a que les den su piquete   hasta albañiles y carpinteros y demás   que se van a distraer de sus obligaciones   je   pero ahí en el ecuador pasa una cosa muy curiosa que es que bueno   hay muchísima cooperación entre todos ¿ves?   Como si todos fueran iguales   ahí las clases sociales se la pelan al sexo ¿verdad?—y todos cooperando para que todos gocen. (201)

> [There you see gentlemen who leave their Galaxie parked outside. They just go to be punched by construction workers, carpenters, and the like, who go there to distract themselves from their duties . . . but there in the Ecuador something funny happens. It is that there is great deal of cooperation amongst them all, right? As if everyone were equal. There, social classes go to hell, sex rules, right?—everyone is helping everyone to enjoy.]

At the bathhouse, social desire for equality is achieved in the collaboration for each person's orgasm, without distinction. In the same way, Adonis' body is a piece of public goods whose purpose is to provide pleasure to the others. Being destined for others abolishes one's own identity and constructs a multifaceted sexuality.

Coercive Sexuality: José Joaquín Blanco

Diametrically opposed to this utopia of the society of pleasure, José Joaquín Blanco's _Púberes Canéforas_ (1983) shows that sexual workers and homosexuals are dominated by individuals whose sexuality consists of inflicting violence on other people's bodies. The novel begins in medias res with the murder of a woman and the kidnapping and the subsequent escape of Felipe: a series of actions to which we are going to discover the keys, one by one, as the plot unravels. Like Adonis, Felipe is a prostitute and, like Maldonado's _mayates_, he has sexual contacts with women too, performing heterosexual acts while failing to desire his homosexual partners. Besides these two aspects that we have already pointed out while analyzing the _mayate_, Felipe is portrayed as a cynical macho who disregards emotions: "no, por el ⟩

amor no me daba" (60) [no, I never intended to love]. Critics are unanimous in their observation that this novel creates a chaotic and miserable atmosphere, representing Mexico City as a pandemonium where *jotos, mayates*, and sex workers are the main victims of the city's social decadence (Pérez 209, Anzaldo *Ciberletras*).

Beyond the joyful machismo of the *mayate* and the *chichifo, Las púberes canéforas* utilizes violence to set the stage for sexuality. As he strolls through the riotous streets of Mexico City's downtown, Guillermo, a homosexual character who previously had an affair with Felipe, reflects on his past and narrates an encounter in a dark corner of the neighborhood where in his climactic moment the *joto* feels "el cañon de una pistola en el cuello, o la navaja y el picahielo en la espina, y se había acabado el amor" (22) [a gun on his neck, or a knife or the ice chopper in the spine, and the loving had finished]. As in the chronicles by Nájera and Novo, the narrative voice navigates the signs of the streets where we meet the most painful bodies. Claudia—who lives with Analía, a prostitute with whom Felipe decides to live as couple—observes that the juniors—wealthy young men—look for a pleasure consisting in "el ejercicio bruto del poder: pagaban para joder, para humillar y pagaban muy poco. Humillar, golpear, insultar, envilecer, hundir, emborracharse de poder, sentirse como dioses" (27) [the brutal exercise of power: they paid to bother, to humiliate, and they paid very little. To humiliate, to beat, to insult, to scorn, to diminish, to get drunk with power, to feel like gods"]. As supremacy and hate are forms of pleasure, pleasure functions as a politics of domination. "The rude exercise of power" is a phrase that transcends the sexual practice and leads to the social dimension. The composition of the novel is a complex allegory that parallels coercion, sexuality, and machismo—or machismo as a coercive sexuality.

Far from the utopia of the society of pleasure we find in *El vampiro de la Colonia Roma* and from the extrapolated lack of desire in *Después de todo, Las púberes canéforas* conveys a type of sexuality that avoids any linkage with the sexual partner, a sexuality diametrically opposed to any eroticism. The enjoyment of killing corresponds to the effeminate subject's fantasy of being a victim of violence. In a drunken moment, Guillermo reminds us of the image of an old man who pays to perform fellatio on a man inside a sordid movie house, receiving the scorn of his sexual partner. Before this scene, La Gorda, his party friend comments: "[e]ntre más crudas, incluso más obscenas, las cosas le parecían menos mentirosas" (42) [While cruder and more obscene, everything seemed less false to him]. In this crudeness, we can find the feature of a sexuality that goes beyond identities encoded in terms of sexual orientation. On the one hand, the perpetrator of violence does not express desire but pours scorn and on the other, the *joto* expects precisely that attitude. Claudia, the prostitute, has identified the macho as a destructive subject, whose enjoyment implies an exercise of physical power over the undesirable body of the hated woman. Therefore, we can propose that the exacerbation of machismo, its ultimate manifestation, is accomplished with misogynist and homophobic violence.

Fleshy Souvenir: Amor Chacal

Even though there is an abundance of reported homophobic crimes perpetrated by *mayates*, this sexual practice has also been represented as festive and even incorporated into the economy of Mexican daily life. In 2001, the documentary video *Amor chacal* [*Chacal* Love] by Juan Carlos Bautista and Víctor Jaramillo won the First Prize of the contest of *Mix de la Diversidad Sexual* for amateur video. Although as a production it is rudimentary, this work succeeds in depicting the mechanisms of seduction of *mayates* and discloses the interstices of a culture encoded with a fecal discourse. The epigraph refers to a substratum of Mexican culture that has not been colonized yet: "[l]a cruz y el hierro destruyeron la antigua cultura, menos el gusto por ese placer" [The cross and the weapons destroyed the ancient culture—except the inclination for that pleasure]. After the epigraph, we hear the voice of Toña la Negra (a Veracruzan singer of boleros) singing "alma de jarocho que nació morena" [soul of a Veracruzan that was born brown skinned] in the background as young men ride their bikes on the streets of a village called Alvarado. This is a racial postcard: those young men are presented, along the most famous local singer, as tourist attractive of the town. The first sequence the video is suggestive of a tourist promotion material. The villagers and visitors from the urban areas interact aiming for homoerotic contact. Tourists bring cameras to focus on and seduce *mayates*, and the latter respond mischievously, disclosing the contradictions of masculinity that fluctuates between patriarchal hegemony and its permissive margins.

The discourse of the villagers is full of fecal images referring to the sexual contact between men. If the fecal signs designate a sexuality characterized by the *mayate-joto* relationship (or *choto*, in the Veracruz's dialect), we notice an eroticization of the residual. The sexuality of the *chacal-joto* occurs in the sedimentary zone. This designation implies an execrable connotation. The sexuality of excretions would then be an abominable and repudiated sexuality. Nevertheless, the fecal is part of public expressions, on the streets, in the cantinas, and in the verses sung by folk singers in the plazas, whose songs are intended to amuse tourists, but not to be transmitted through the media. The fecal can be interpreted as a field of resistance whose representations, besides referring to a form of homoeroticism, lets us glimpse a clandestine—although visible— aspect of masculinity. As we have observed before, the *mayate* does not challenge the norms of masculine sexuality. We can find support for this contention in the interviews with Alvarado's neighbors. Homoerotic practice is admissible under certain conditions: (a) no condemning judgments: "nadie dice nada"; "nadie tiene por qué meterse contigo" [nobody says anything; nobody has a reason to interfere in your business]; (b) generalization: "en Alvarado el que no es puto es mayate" [in Alvarado, he who is not a *joto* is a *mayate*]; (c) amusement: "aquí todos somos muy alegres"; "es puro desmadre"; "es que nos gusta el relajo"; "¿quieres cotorrear?" [here everybody is very relaxed; it is just fun; we just like to enjoy ourselves; would you like to have fun?]; (d) tourist service: "al cliente lo que pida"; "todo el que llega a Alvarado, viene buscando mayate" [we do whatever the costumer asks for; everyone who visits Alvarado is looking for a *mayate*].

The absence of condemning judgment does not mean that the moral and religious discourses justify this sexuality; it means that disciplinary apparatuses fail to change it coercively. Unspeakable, nefarious sin under canon law erupts in representations of fecal homoeroticism in Alvarado's daily life. Through the fecal, the judgment remains subsumed under mechanisms of the comic discourse, which disempowers condemnation, although it does not abolish the hierarchy of the *mayate* over the *joto*. The generalization that classifies men in two categories ("el que no es puto es mayate"), actually reiterates the macho-effeminate hierarchy; thus heterosexual norms constrain homoeroticism. Patriarchal norms are reiterated in the homoerotic relationships as a sort of parody that confirms rather than questions the heterosexual institution. But this reiteration happens in a liminal space. Liminal activities, as defined by J.W. Lett, are at the same time accepted and delegitimated: "Liminoid activities, in short, are those socially accepted and approved activities which seem to deny or ignore the legitimacy of the institutionalised statuses, roles, norms, values, and rules of everyday, 'ordinary' life" (cit. in Ryan 102). The *mayate*'s sexuality is accepted regardless of its fecal image, as long as he displays machismo. The fecal motif as a core of the *mayate* image destabilizes eroticism. It transgresses the explicit rules of sexuality that conceal a clandestine code, unwritten, and stricken from public discourses. Thus, the folk singer who sings, "Mi lenguaje es malacate/ todo el que viene a Alvarado/ viene buscando mayate" [My language is vulgar/ but everyone who comes to Alvarado/ is looking for a *mayate*], takes a position far removed from politeness. His presence in the open space of the tourist party is a moment that suspends law. Here the oral discourse in Alvarado constructs the *mayate* as a product for tourist consumption.

Los mayates form a community that privileges enjoyment as its income and doing so confers on it public recognition. This economic status transgress the patriarchal norm and, as Zizek says, discussing the preeminence of superego over written law: "[w]hat 'holds together' a community most deeply is not so much identification with the Law that regulates the community's 'normal' everyday circuit, but rather *identification with specific forms of transgression of the Law, of the Law's suspension* (in psychoanalytic terms, with a specific form of *enjoyment*)" (1994, 55; emphasis in original). Folk singers and *mayates* challenge the social norm to propose a consuetudinary type of pleasure. Homoeroticism does not mean the tragic transgression of an individual who breaks the social norm and fights against, or is a victim of disciplinary apparatuses that would characterize a hero of psychological novels. The generalization that includes all the villagers and collective leisure on the streets and on the beaches seems to erase any conflict between patriarchal law and sociosexual practices. Contrary to the tensions in the bourgeois novel and melodrama, this quotidian farce escapes psychological density. *Mayates* do not express any identity conflict; they have nothing to hide, and nobody has any reason to judge them, as is made clear from some of their statements such as "That's fun," "Some of my friends do it, some of them don't," and "There is nothing bad about that."

Permissiveness leads to ritualized homoerotic contacts. It establishes the rationale that liberates the subject from guilt through a double standard regulated collectively (a regulation needs nothing more than a gesture of complicity). This means that the double standard is an implicit way of ordering and signifying masculinity in the body of the *mayate*. In Patricia Ponce's ethnographic work on Boca del Cielo, a coastal town in the state of Veracruz, she finds that the difference between the *choto* and women is the ability to seduce heterosexual men: unlike *chotos*, women are not supposed to court men; they are educated to be receptacles of masculine will (119). On the other hand, *jotos*

[g]ustan tener relaciones sexuales con varones heterosexuales, no con homosexuales, y en la cama prefieren ser penetrados . . . no conciben relaciones homoeróticas, es decir, que a un varón le guste otro varón, si esto sucede es que son chotos reprimidos; consideran que a los verdaderos hombres les debe gustar solamente las mujeres. (133)

[They like to have sex with heterosexual men, who are not homosexuals. The [*jotos*] prefer to be penetrated . . . they don't conceive that a man likes them; if that happens then their partner is a repressed *choto*; they consider that true men like only women.]

The *choto*'s active role as a seducer and the *mayate*'s lack of attraction for the *choto* are the main factors that differentiate heterosexuality from homosexuality. The topic of the song *El pato* ["The Duck," which in some Caribbean regions is another derogatory word for effeminate homosexuals], sung in the last sequence of *Amor chacal* by la negra Graciana (a popular singer in Veracruz City) emphasizes the distribution of roles between *chotos* and *mayates.* In the song the duck (the *joto*) pretends to receive fellatio, which according to Patricia Ponce is a privilege of the *mayate.* Then the *mayate* reaffirms his top role. An old mulatto woman plays the harp and sings a song abounding in graphic fecal references, in the middle of the Plaza in Veracruz City, in the morning. The fecal image reinforces the lack of attractiveness of the *choto.* This is a relationship between enjoyment and domination. The one who receives fellatio dominates, penetrates, repudiates the effeminate, who at least has to pay for the beers at the cantina. *Mayates* are always trying to avoid being penetrated because as some of them recognize, they are afraid of enjoying it. Fecality is also a form of pleasure; they even celebrate a private contest named "el mojón de oro" [The golden piece of shit].

Despite the social complicity with *mayates, Amor chacal* does not focus on homoerotic relationships among villagers. Even in the conversations with local transvestites, the only subject is sexual contacts with visitors. According to Juan Carlos Bautista, the video is a travel journal, a private record, or a chronicle of encounters between urban men and coastal exotic bodies. He says, "se trata de mostrar la liberalidad, alegría, desparpajo, de los muchachos veracruzanos, muy distinta del comportamiento sexual de la mayoría de los mexicanos" (interview, July 2002) [it is about showing the liberality, contentment, and abandon of Veracruzans, sexual behavior very different from most Mexicans]. In Veracruz, the object of desire, the *chacal,* is key to the economic exchange between tourists and villagers. From the song by Toña la Negra about the Veracruzans' exoticism to the shots of young men in Alvarado with their hands touching their genitals, dancing seminaked in the cabins at the beach, as well as the folk singers who refer openly to homoeroticism with fecal images, it is evident that the stereotyped mestizo or mulatto is a profitable sexual object. The search for this sexual object is also an ethnographic trip provided that it collects and communicates "cultural experiences."[2] Let us understand "cultural experience" as consumption of otherness conceived as valuable in terms of sex and ethnicity, as Jacqueline Sánchez Taylor points out in her work on sexual tourism in the Caribbean region (42). Therefore it is evident that the exaltation of local forms of life is a way to stage ethnicity for the "master" visitor, on whom a significant part of the economy depends. The expression "al cliente lo que pida" [we do whatever the costumer asks for] implies this staging of daily life for the tourists' eyes. To sell cultural experiences becomes a sort of collective imperative for most of the interviewed. "Aquí hay de todo" [here there is everything], "nadie se ha quejado de los muchachos de Alvarado" [nobody has complained about the boys from Alvarado] are phrases that describe a product. Sexuality as a tourist attraction is a cultural commodity in the diverse market of the global economy. Bodies, as well as food and archeological sites, are symbolic merchandise included in the Veracruzan tourist offerings.

We can interpret traditional homoeroticism and its promotion as another form of symbolic richness that official programs of cultural institutions propose to preserve: to keep the cultural roots, the forms, and customs that constitute identity. Based on this principle, the image of *mayate* does not contradict hegemony, as long as it derives, at least indirectly, from the cultural staging of the institutions. The imperative to reinforce tradition has, on the one hand, a nationalistic background—meaning the expressions that identify the hometown community rather than the nation (Stavenhagen 23). Displaying *chacales* as constituents of Veracruzan amusement and permissiveness promotes the idea of a paradise of pleasure, and refers at the same time to a collective identity as a product for tourist consumption. It reinscribes the local into the global. Hence, tourism is a simulacrum that colonizes the national. In other words, the discourse of the national remains in use as long as it can be integrated as a performance executed to satisfy the enjoyment of the visitors.

9

The Invisible Man: Masculinity and Violence

This chapter discusses the difficulties, in recent years, of defining violent men. By studying specific works of drama and film that deal with this topic, I identify the relationship between the global order and misogyny as reflected by the feminicides that have occurred since 1993 in Ciudad Juárez, a city located across the U.S.-Mexico border from El Paso, Texas. In this context, the violent man is available as a representation for which an actual referent is always hidden from the public eye by creating scapegoats or disseminating elusive arguments. Making visible the concealed is a task that the study of gender representation and globalization attempts to perform. With this analysis I complete my study of masculinity related to the national state by proposing a global contextualization of masculinity.

Violence as a System

In March 2002, demonstrators arrive in Ciudad Juárez culminating a march that had begun a week earlier in Chihuahua City. They bear a cross adorned with feminine objects. A wide black fabric connects the heads of a group of marching women in pink hats. They sing a monotonous song with the slogan "Ni una más" [not one more], reminiscent of funeral chants. After them, a large group wearing masks recites verses from *The Trojans* by Aeschylus. The masks are monstrously tragic, as in the classic theater, and the chorus produces a commotion as it utters its powerful diatribe. Painful manifestations of Christian funeral rituals and laments of Greek tragedy reinscribe Western cultural metaphors in a forum that has placed violence at the center of public attention. The waves of homicide have gathered diverse political positions and social strati. Bloody masks represent the victims and the group of women tied with the black fabric represents the mothers. From the beginning of the last decade of the twentieth century, both victims and mothers have been clearly visible in the public sphere. They have played a leading part in resisting violence. By 2002, more than 300 female corpses with traces of sexual cruelty had been found in the desert and even in urban locations around Ciudad Juárez and the rest of Chihuahua. These victims have often been described as poor, young, maquiladora workers, thus raising a question about the socioeconomic context of these murders.

Innocent, sacrificed women are the central motif of a discourse of martyrdom that has been enunciated from the most diverse social actors in Mexico and beyond: journalists, politicians, organizational, and religious leaders, as well as academics, intellectuals, and artists. *El silencio que la voz de todas quiebra* [The Silence that Breaks the Voices of All Women] by Rohry Benítez et al. (1999), *Las muertas de Juárez* [Juárez's Dead Women] by Víctor Ronquillo (1999), *Huesos en el desierto* (2002) [Bones in the Desert] by Sergio González Rodríguez, *Desert Blood-Juárez Murders* by Alicia Gaspar de Alba (2005), as well as documentaries such as *Señorita Extraviada* [Lost Girl] directed by Lourdes Portillo (2001) and *La batalla de las cruces* [The Battle of the Crosses] directed by Rafael Bonilla (2005), among many others, testify to and document—that is, portray—those killings as a politics of victimization that is occurring in a way that seems to be criminal, but not political. They reflect on the murders from a political perspective, providing martyrdom with a meaning in the field of power relationships. Their representation of victims corresponds to what authorities and the most conservative social sectors declared in the first place: these women caused their own victimization; they provoked the perpetrator; they got what they deserved. Such declarations provoked from various sources a reaction that portrayed the murdered women as pure victims whom society labels as scapegoats.

Paradoxically, this violence seems to be unmotivated; hence the figure of the perpetrator is presented as a monstrous, exceptional individual. While the images of corpses are reiterated, discourses become radicalized, mythologizing death and then postponing the political fight against violence. Narratives accumulate symbolic values and nurture ideologies and imaginaries. To think about victims and perpetrators in a sacrificial system dehistoricizes and depoliticizes violence. The concept of myth by Roland Barthes, consisting of a naturalizing and essentialized discourse, leads us to make a deconstructive reading that dismantles the assumptions that outline the myths of victim and perpetrator (Barthes 337–341). Thus, the authorities delegitimize the critics of impunity while perpetuating the myth of inevitable victimization. Government actions prove that nothing can be done to fight violence and that victimization is therefore an inexorable social destiny. Yet, when these critics extrapolate the perpetrator-victim relationship in moral terms, that is, the perpetrator as a monster and the victim as a saint, they also participate in the construction of social myths of violence and sacrifice.

The sacrificial system guarantees the continuity of the violent order, which benefits a murderer who remains unrepresented, while the victim is excessively visible. In the case of Ciudad Juárez's feminicides, we can describe this sacrificial system as follows:

1. Murderers have a hidden identity aided by their impunity, which points to a complicity between perpetrators and judicial agents.
2. Victims are characterized as morally impeccable, and as marginalized for being immigrants, women, mestizas or Indians, and poor.
3. Victims are not enemies of perpetrators but bodies on which the latter inscribe signs to be decoded by unknown addressees. In other words, there are actions that seem to be signifying, but there are no clues as to what they communicate.
4. Perpetrators are substituted by scapegoats based on false evidence, torture, and media campaigns. This not only conceals the meaning of victimization, but also "officially" constructs the perpetrator to blur the identity of the murderers.

The most reiterated interpretation of these murders is based on a gender approach, where it is assumed that perpetrators are men and victims are women. Then, the feminine and the masculine determine the characterization in this plot of violence. Whereas perpetrators are invisible, victims are over-represented in social discourses. On the one hand, a complex web of complicity plays a central role in the perpetrators' invisibility. And on the other, activists, journalists, artists, and academics invest most of their resources in the overrepresentation of the victim. Identity politics is thus the agency that produces the knowledge of violence as a gender-determined phenomenon. But here identification is focused on the construction of the victim's body (which reaches the status of allegorical representation of society as victim) and fails to offer convincing characterizations of perpetrators. The murder is a confusing trace, an equivocal mark on the body of victims.

The violent agent is reduced to a mark of masculine gender in narratives related to the assassination of women. Thus, violence must be a constituent characteristic of imagining maleness. In the dramaturgy and cinema of the border region produced in recent years, the construction of masculinities related to violence aims to make visible what seems to be invisible; or at least the representation of invisible finds intelligibility in the interpretive frame of gender. Visibility and invisibility become questions of gender definitions. Masculine violence tends to disappear from the identifiable, which cannot be interpreted as the disappearance of the agent of violence; rather it denotes the lack of adequate resources to achieve agency, socioeconomic profile, paths of dissemination and empowerment, and all the other aspects that would lead us to understand this characterization.

In films and plays related to the feminicides, we can distinguish two trends in the perpetrator's characterization: the socioeconomic contextualization of the violent manhood and the construction of men as monsters. Men who lack the economic resources to provide for their family, and the development of furtive and killing skills among teenage gangs, police, and drug dealers, reinforces the characterization of men raised in the environment of unemployment and organized crime. These men are sociological depictions that explain violent actions and are the most likely rationalizations of the male condition. But this determinist approach to these men's violence is continually questioned by the emergence of the monster image, forged at the point of the sublime, that is, the ineffable, the Kantian sublime, understood as the terror of the incomprehensible and monstrous (Kant 1982, 21). But this sublime is not a consequence of a finite rationality or the uselessness of words for attaining the truth, as we can find in thinkers such as Wittgenstein; it is not, in short, a metaphysical question, but a question of the production of images that concern the politics of terror.

Behind the actions of criminals, authorities, journalists, activists, and so on, there is a symbolic context consisting of moral, political, and economic interests and beliefs that needs to be decoded if we are to understand how the system of killing has reached the pinnacle of sovereignty. Provided that killing is form of control, learning to kill would seem a valuable skill. If Néstor García Canclini could say that citizenship is the condition for a democratic state and that a regime dominated by the market is a society of consumption (1995, 29), we can also suggest that a regime of violence defines a collectivity in terms of perpetrators and victims. A regime of violence consists of a system of destruction, a protocol of complicity, methods of coercion, and a code of revenge and blackmail: systems, methods, protocol, and codes denote violence as a complex apparatus of norms that has been expanded and consolidated by a learning process. Thus, the monster image that results from this training can be taken as a simulacrum. We have to argue that violence cannot be an irrational phenomenon; rather, it is a rationalization of abuse and control. This rationality constitutes a quotidian politics expressed in language, use of space, and forms of social interactions.

To impart competence in dealing with this system of violence, the education of men focuses on the development of a technology of destruction. This discipline is outside of the official institutions that control bodies, that is, the school, the factory, and so on. This education follows models of identity that emerge in the realm of daily life. A society dominated by fear has to create victims and perpetrators. They are there, and we are reluctant to recognize their presence because it is intolerable to admit that violence rather than a number of lamentable occurrences is, as a matter of fact, a codified system of behavior, an economy, and a process of political struggle. To steal, to rape, to fight, and to exterminate are procedures; they require initiation rites and permissible spaces. They are not just a series of activities emerging as the subalterns' tactics of resistance. They are forms of learning generated in the channels of cultural dissemination. If the press grows complacent toward the scandals and depiction of horror, then bloody actions profitably feed the public demand for hyperrealist experiences; if complicity is important to protect life, then toleration and silence become virtues; blackmail and coercion are forms of negotiation for both criminals and politicians.

A large number of plays written on border issues show us how masculinity is reshaped in the context of violence. To quote a few examples, in Manuel Talavera Trejo's *Novenario* (1994) the only male child of the family lacks the resources to take care of himself, and Antonio Zúñiga's *El gol de oro* (1999) [The Golden Goal] shows the gang's furtive stalking and escapes, and stages the education of males in the context of unemployment and criminal labor. Although these works do not describe characters that we can call perpetrators, they allow us to view a system of values and virtues that legitimate violent events. They show masculinities that can be known only in relation to the globalized culture and economy of the Mexico-U.S. border.

In Manuel Talavera Trejo's *Novenario*, the mother's ghost spies on the actions of her children during the novena (nine days) after her death. She is concerned about the precarious condition of her unemployed son Chema. Chema, however, imagines a brilliant future for himself as a rock star. But he is only a dependant of his sisters employed in a maquiladora. The mother's ghost reacts with shivers each time Chema says he will be a great man (Talavera 11–12). What are the prospects of an unemployed young man in a working-class neighborhood placed in the ephemeral globalized economy?

Antonio Zúñiga's *El gol de oro* proposes an answer. Two *cholos* (young gang members) are waiting for the bus. While waiting they play with the glasses they had earlier snatched from a blind man called Epi. The police arrive and search them until they find a package of drugs. The *cholos* sell drugs in the maquiladora. This basic scene of a popular neighborhood sketches the economy of narcotics. The police agents detain the *cholos* in order to recover the drug for their own business. The police score a goal; they win in the game of drug-related power. "Being a great man" in this context is to dominate in the struggle for control of the drug market. The microcosmic view of *El gol de oro* presents us with a sociological interpretation of violent masculinity. After their exclusion from domestic space and "legal" employment, men become protagonists of the story of underground economy. Violence is a way to survive the expulsion from the "formal" economy and the normative way of life. If he does not belong to the legitimated spaces, he has no power, that is, he is no longer considered a social actor and he is not morally or politically authorized to follow logic. A violent subject can then be defined as a subject who lacks political privileges and credibility but possesses force and benefits from the structure of the underground economy. It is force without power, a contradiction that leads us to understand the emergence of the violent male image.

Violence perpetrated by men can be interpreted as eagerness to recover lost power. It is then conceived as a precariousness rather than the exercise of power. *Cuentas pendientes* (1992) [Unsettled Accounts] by Tomás Chacón characterizes a subject who is violent in this sense. The scene is the living room in an apartment where three women live. One of them, Carmen, has left her husband and children because of domestic violence. As the drama develops it dismantles the tidy and organized stage of the opening sequences until it becomes a torture room. Eduardo, the husband, comes over to punish her for her *cuentas pendientes*—her unsettled accounts. The language employed in the title refers to an economy of violence. Carmen has left her family, and so Eduardo is offended. Because Eduardo claims to be the victim of her abandonment, he threatens her with his gun, and finally beats her. Throughout the play, Eduardo drinks alcohol, which adds clumsiness to his character. Clumsiness exalts violence. However, we cannot consider violence as merely irrational behavior. As we observe in this piece, violence is the culminating action of a discourse of domination. Eduardo comes to claim his lost power, to recover his realm, and establish his rules oriented to inflict on Carmen physical and non-physical damage. The statement of the rules and the violent actions that support it are the two main components of what we can call a politics of enjoyment in line with the political notion proposed by

Zizek. Enjoyment is entitlement, possession, and domination; enjoyment is an absolute control of the other to the point of deciding her life and death (Zizek 1993, 203). After establishing his dominance by injuring Carmen, Eduardo turns to address her with affectionate and tender language: "my little girl," "little dove." He adopts a protective stance and dictates the condition of her confinement.

> Tú sabes de lo que soy capaz. (Se le acerca) Vamos a mejorar las cosas, no es bueno que andes fuera de casa, así nomás. Tu sitio está conmigo y tus hijos. (Le acaricia el rostro) Les va a dar mucho gusto verte. Yo jamás . . . jamás les he dicho que eres una perra. (La besa y la manosea.) Ellos sólo saben que eres una pobrecita oveja descarriada, pero nada más. (15)

> [You know what I am capable of. (He approaches her.) We will improve things; it is not good that you are away from home, just because. Your place is with your children and with me. (He caresses her face.) They will be happy to see you. I never . . . never have told them you are a bitch. (He kisses and touches her.) They only know you are a poor strayed sheep, but not more.]

Eduardo seduces and forces her to go to the bedroom with him. The mixture of blows and caresses constitute a coercive sexuality. Family values justify his beating. Thus morality grounds Chacón's depiction of domestic violence. The first act of *Cuentas pendientes* suggests that the patriarchal system legitimates beating women. Here to legitimate is to convert violence into discourse. Violence is articulated as an event that at the same time functions as a sign, provided that it is incorporated in the symbolic exchange by carrying out threats and imposing a lesson of domination. Phrases like "sólo a golpes entiendes" [you only understand with blows] imply that violence is a learning process. While the torturer or the rapist attains his imposing position, he and his victims are involved in an exchange of meanings. The moment she voluntarily executes acts he expects her to perform, total domination is achieved. That is, when the victim internalizes the norm, she has learned to be a victim as an existential condition. Coercion as discourse legitimizes the codification of violent relationships.

To Write Means to Injure

In the representations that circulate in the public arena about victimized bodies, it is evident that violence is an act of writing: injuries are both aggressions on the body and marks to be read. Newspaper crime reports and forensic records unfold a narrative of scars and traces that involve messages encoded with the methods of injury, fetishes, and sites of abuse. Understanding violence is basically a hermeneutic task practiced within the community where violence becomes a form of communication. This communication is possible under the logic of sacrifice. Torture, beating, rape, and killing acquire the status of cultural practice—or *habitus* in Bourdieu's terms (1990, 53)—when reiterated, learned, and disseminated: in short, violence is incorporated into the symbolic order that certifies norms, that is, it has achieved the status of norm. An order of violence is one where killing has become a series of rituals and discourses. Violence is a prolific source of representations; it is part of daily life; it has its procedures; and it is interpreted.

Estrellas enterradas (2001) [Buried Stars] by Antonio Zúñiga is staged with a series of tropes—fetishes, icons, allegories—that have also been incorporated into the narratives about serial murders of women in Ciudad Juárez from 1993 to the present. Teófilo a 30-year-old electrician, and Obed, his adolescent assistant, work on the electricity poles in the desert. The poles' cross-shaped shadows are crucial in the stage composition: the logic of sacrifice we have seen in the march "Ni una más" is here reiterated by the inclusion again of the foundational sacrificial symbol of Christianity. Obed carries a bagful of women's shoes with him each time they have to move to another post. They lay and connect wires. The dialogue between Teófilo, Obed, the voice on the radio, and the ghosts of the dead women deploys a multileveled spatial structure that juxtaposes the actual scenery of the work place (the desert and the poles), with the site of the stage where the voices of the radio are emitted and with the invisible space of the ghosts perceived by Obed, but hidden from Teófilo. The voice in the radio not only provides directions for laying and connecting wires but

also conveys a second meaning that refers to the procedures of raping and killing:

> ¡Tú nomás anota! Motor desigual a más no poder, al encontrar pareja
> conectar de volada. Luego virar al norte, allá está lo bueno, ¿entendido?
> Cinco postes al punto. En el quinto conectar y esperar la corriente que
> llega . . . Mucha atención en el quinto, porque no hay quinto malo y si
> te truena, te truena, ¿entendido? ¡Cambio! (25)

> [You just take note! Extremely uneven motor, upon finding a match,
> connect it immediately. Then turn to the north where the good stuff is,
> do you understand? When you have five poles ready, you must wait at
> the fifth one for the current to arrive . . . Attention to the fifth, because
> there is not a bad fifth, if it breaks, it just breaks, do you understand?
> Change!]

Using the jargon of radio communication, these instructions fluc-
tuate between the semantic fields of electricity and victimization.
The phrase "extremely uneven motor" directs our attention to the
social basis of victimization and invokes the context of unequal
social relationships. Unequal machinery or the machinery of
inequality functions effectively. "Upon finding a match, connect
them immediately" describes abduction and rape. The allusion to
the north connotes migratory movements. This semantic ambiguity
produces a historical and geographic dimension to the killing of
women. Establishing unequal connections in the desert, where
people migrate, and describing those connections with the verb "to
break" imply the rape of immigrants. The colloquial phrase "no
hay quinto malo" expresses that no virginity can be rejected.
"Tronar," which literally means to explode, refers in Mexican colloquial language to a brutal defloration or to a murder.

As in the piece by Chacón, rape is part of a system rather than
an exceptional event. In *Estrellas enterradas* rape is represented in
terms of procedures; it is an action governed by certain rules, a
behavior system codified to the point of normalizing a violent sexuality, the practice of a form of desire in which the central condition is the elimination of the victim. The actions of the perpetrator
are encoded to exercise domination. Therefore, domination is the
object of desire. If the work of Teófilo and Obed consists of bringing electricity to the desert, this seems to allegorize the expansion

of masculine control. Throughout the play the ghosts of killed women appear, although only Obed and the audience perceive them. At the end we learn that Teófilo has raped and killed Obed's sister. While Obed suffers hallucinations and Teófilo considers him demented, the latter is sober and rational. This detail proves that violence has, without doubt, a rational component. The bringing of electricity and the maintenance of patriarchal rationality summarize the metaphoric basis of *Estrellas enterradas*. Associating rationality with violence allows us to explore a deconstruction of the discourses that establish concepts and norms supporting masculine supremacy.

Technologies of Masculine Violence

The construction of masculine supremacy depends on what Teresa de Lauretis calls "technologies of gender." This term conveys production and machinery, a metaphor that has been useful in describing the processes of modern civilization, which is the process of disseminating images that are convincing or seductive. Based on this metaphor we can conceive of the male image as a product that is introduced by the image industries and reproduced in the social life. The violent man is then a notion constructed and disseminated in the market of images.

In the grocery stores in Ciudad Juárez, among CDs of *narco-corridos* and *cumbias norteñas*, it is possible to find a series of low-quality films referring to feminicides in this city, such as *Las muertas de Juárez* [Juárez's Dead Women] (directed by Enrique Murillo, 2002), *16 en la lista* [16 in the List] (directed by Roberto Rodobertti, 2001) and *Espejo Retrovisor* [Rear View Mirror] (directed by Héctor Molinar, 2002). They are melodramas based on Manichean stories where heroic police agents persecute murderers and protect decent families of the middle class. Society is depicted as a victim of drug traffickers, smugglers, and the despised poor. Although there is no a definite aesthetic or explicit political orientation, the characters of the violent melodrama are instruments of a political discourse based on the distribution of feelings and morals. Each film proposes a different perpetrator: a mentally disturbed figure, an extravagant man of power, and a despised lower-class criminal. The victims are innocent, defenseless and passive characters that function as sacrificial bodies. In these films, domestic violence, marginalization, and organized crime are the main sources of criminality.

In *Las muertas de Juárez* a smuggler kidnaps women who hire him to cross the border. He takes them to the basement of a maquiladora factory where the entrepreneur rapes and kills them. Police agents are pressed by public opinion and have to find a suspect. A female agent who investigates nightclubs pretending she is a prostitute meets two possible murderers: a Lebanese man and a band of drug dealers. They are detained and confess under torture. In the investigation, the police find the smuggler but the entrepreneur kills him in the end. In a flashback during the rape and assassination of a woman, the entrepreneur recalls events of his childhood: he saw his mother committing adultery, and then he saw how his father punished his mother. The film proposes these childhood remembrances as causes of his misogyny. In a happy ending, the prostitute-agent finds the entrepreneur and the police easily resolve the case.

Accordingly, this violent character is produced because he witnessed his parents practicing adultery and violence. Then he punishes his mother in the body of each woman he victimizes. The adultery of his mother has damaged him emotionally to the point of preventing him from achieving pleasure. Sexuality becomes destructivity. The breakup of his parents causes him to kill women. Although his father was also an adulterer, the entrepreneur does not punish men, only women. He is a reflection of his father. The film is based on the following statements: a) the murderer performs the role of punishing all women for the adultery of the mother; b) loyalty avoids violence against men; c) breaking the patriarchal norms causes the violence. The police, as in the most common thrillers, fight the murders, while civil society's protest against the police ineffectiveness is presented as a factor that obstructs its mission. This film, therefore, reiterates a conservative view by proposing that rescuing the traditional family and coercive institutions is necessary for recovering social harmony.

The main contradiction about misogynist violence can be expressed as follows: on the one hand, it is proposed that traditional family values and patriarchal institutions are detonators of violence, as we observed in the works by Tomás Chacón and Antonio Zúñiga; on the other hand, there is the belief that supporting patriarchy reduces violence. Faith in the order, expressed by the figure of the father or his institutional expression, the police, has nurtured most of the popular interpretations of masculine violence. Like *Las muertas de Juárez*, the film *16 en la lista* celebrates the police institution. In one of the initial sequences, a group of children playing a game where police persecute drug-traffickers actually finds a girl's dead body. This sequence summarizes the dynamics of the whole film. The hero, Charlie, is a young police agent who confronts the drug cartel. His adoptive father is the chief of police. Denise, Charlie's stepsister, is a lawyer who is reluctantly defending two men apprehended for trafficking drugs. Throughout the film, all hints suggest that the murder of women represents a form of challenge by the drug-dealers to the police. Nevertheless, a physician, whom Charlie interviews, describes the murderer as a man "whose reasoning is different than ours, and so he is highly dangerous." In fact, the killer is a psychopath who has personal reasons to kidnap and murder women: they always rejected him, and so killing them is a way of revenge. In a predictable ending, Denise is going to be raped when Charlie shows up to rescue her.

Resentment against women is the main root of violence for these two films. The ghosts of women (as in the Jungian shadow) appear in retrospect, as an adulterer or unloving individuals. Hence, they are presented as the cause of their victimization. The search for motives in the killing of women leads to a rationalization of hate. The image of the perpetrator, now visible, is frightful and perturbing, frightful because it speaks of imminent actions (isn't realism the form for representing imminent actions?), and perturbing because it rationalizes what is abject and consequently makes violence sensible. In the image of the violent man we find this rationalized sense in the fear of the male body. Whereas in organized crime, killing takes part in a code of honor, in killing women the most propagated image is a monster that possesses a dangerous rationality. The serial killer is a pathological subject whose violence is caused by the lack of love that women are expected to provide with abnegation to men. Thus violence against women, including murder, is understood as an entitlement because women fail to perform the role that the patriarchy has designated to them.

Espejo retrovisor further rationalizes the violence, introducing the social-class factor to the characterization of the murderer. The story of a boy who earns money by washing windshields parallels that of a middle class girl. They have never talked but have seen each other several times. In the end he kidnaps, rapes, and kills her. The melodramatic extrapolation of the middle-class victim and the marginal perpetrator draws a dividing line between those who are socially healthy and those who grow up with resentment against the former.

It is important to underline that these films do not condemn all violent actions. The police and the men related to the victims kill and destroy justifiably. These works consider violence as actions against the masculine tutelage over feminine bodies. Hence, they interpret violence as an action affecting the possession of women bodies rather than affecting women's bodies as such. Narratives of violence show a concern for the constitution of male violence and consider victims as the arena of battle between men.

The Killer Man is a Killer State

The documentary *Señorita Extraviada* by Lourdes Portillo highlights two types of violent men, the police and organized criminals, as well as two types of victims, the murdered women and the scapegoats presented by authorities as perpetrators. As in the film *Las muertas de Juárez*, Portillo proposes the context of maquiladoras as the crime scene. Violence follows the Marxist theory of economic determination of social phenomenon, particularly regarding the disempowerment of men by unemployment that produces criminals (as we can see also in works by Talavera Trejo and Antonio Zúñiga mentioned earlier). The shortage of employment for men has expelled them from privileges within the family and forced them to enroll in organized crime. The documentary *Juárez: desierto de esperanza* by Cristina Michaus (2002), points to the displacement of men from employment as the cause of hatred against women. If a socioeconomic phenomenon produces violence, the thesis that popular films propose about the psychopath must be false. In this socioeconomic hypothesis a monster is not the one enclosed behind the scenes but rather a patriarchal politics for controlling bodies. That is, the murderer is not identified because concealing him is precisely a strategy that serves a politics of fear. A large part of the film by Michaus presents the testimony of a woman apprehended with her husband because of a fight with neighbors. Police agents sexually abuse her after they show her pictures of policemen raping, torturing, and killing women. The most widely disseminated image of misogynist violence (and we have as reference a number of chronicles, testimonies, literary works, films, and TV and Radio programs) stages the murder in parties where men consume psychotropic substances and gang-rape a woman who is finally killed and disposed of in a visible site. Society fears these images of perpetrators who enjoy the invisibility provided by the impunity and the complicity of public institutions.

The image of the male killer corresponds to the image of a criminal state: both are characterized by invisibility. The system that makes murderers invisible and false murderers or scapegoats visible defines a form of authoritarian state based on the ability to show and hide bodies. Authorities establish an official truth about murders according to interests that are hidden from public perception. To govern is to make unobjectionable declarations about what should be visible. Hanna Arendt calls authoritarian the system in which the authority's word is identified as law (1976, 462–463). The state that this law produces is a state of terror. In this sense the state's role, rather than being passive before criminality, is an active factor in establishing strategic truths instrumental to the elimination of democratic consensus and society's defense resources. Against the view of several journalistic, documentary, and literary works that point to the police as one of the main perpetrators of violence against women, and also related to organized crime, the former governor of Chihuahua Patricio Martínez stated in December 2003 that the killers of women come from the lower classes. Accordingly, federal and local governments have increased the police force to fight violence and target gang members, homosexuals, and countercultural youth. If however, most analytical and testimonial works perceive the police as the violent male image, increasing its force merely results in expanding the violence.

Films such as *Las muertas de Juárez* and *16 en la lista* concur with the declarations of officials, conceiving violent men as psychopaths who have suffered the breakdown of patriarchal principles: lack of women's love for men and their expulsion from the leading position in the family. In the documentary *Juárez: desierto de esperanza* Ester Chávez Cano, the leader of the organization "Casa Amiga" devoted to assisting women who are victims of domestic violence says, "faltarán siglos para que el hombre entienda que el poder que ha recibido del patriarcado no es para destruir sino para acompañar" [it will take centuries for men to finally understand that the power they have received from the patriarchy is not to destroy but to accompany]. This means, finally, that popular films, leaders of civil society, and officials, all situate the source of violence not in the patriarchy, but in its noncompliance.

In contrast, most documentaries, testimonies, and literary works conceive of violence not as a failure of the patriarchy, but as its ineffectiveness. Patriarchy produces violence as a strategy for keeping its hegemony. This strategy includes the invisibility of killers, the indolence of politicians, the complacency of the media, and the overwhelming climate of fear. Nevertheless, this politics of invisibility does not necessarily lead to the reestablishment of male supremacy, as it may be only a symptom of its own breakdown. It is desirable that violence motivates a general counter-reaction to defend and preserve life, the most ethical principle that humanity has ever conceived. Daring to think that this countermovement is possible is daring to think that maleness can be liberated from the constraints of the patriarchy. But can it be and will it ever be? That is the question.

Notes

2 Sense of Sensuality

1. From here onward the terms *modernismo* (noun) and *modernista* (adjective) will be used in Spanish and they refer to the literary and artistic movement that took place in Spanish America and Spain from the 1880s to 1910s.

2. Here the term formalization is used to designate reiterated practices that become consuetudinary, and finally named and represented, hence codified within a cultural dimension. Formalization is deeply rooted in the constitution of symbolic systems: it can be understood in terms of *habitus* of representation, in the notion of Pierre Bourdieu (1990, 88); or we can refer to the reiteration as a form that is produced as a question that matters, a question that merges into the flux of senses, to use Judith Butler's terms. Both conceptions centralize body as the source that generates symbolical systems.

3. Another issue that is apparent in the presentation of the male body as sign of modernity is the ethnicity of who is represented in the public. Even in contemporary Mexico, representing white bodies is still a practice that floods media and art. European images are proposed as beautiful. It is perfectly evident that mestizo Mexicans are not looking at themselves on the public stage. The white body is seen as the desired body; in other words it is the colonization of beauty. A matter of masks is then ruling the appreciation of male nudity.

4. Néstor García Canclini conceives Latin American modernity as a juxtaposition of temporalities or "Multi-temporal heterogeneity", which redefines tradition into the dynamics of modern society (García Canclini 1990, 72).

5. With this expression, we try to rephrase what Connell conceives as the language of the body, when pointing out the independence of the body orientations from the social discourses of identity (93–96).

6. The paintings of *castas* were popular during the colonial Spanish American period. They are depictions of the racial categories and their roles in that society. They can be considered, as we suggest here, the precursors of the ethnographic art and literature of the nineteenth century in Spain and Spanish America, called *costumbrismo*, a descriptive style that is focused on the customs.

3   The Perturbing Dress: Transvestism in Visual arts

1. This nonopposite logic of cross-dressing leads us to the conception of transvestism as a reconciliation by double identification that Jossianna Arroyo-Martínez uses for defining "cultural transvestism" (20).

4   Intimacy in the War: The Revolutionary Desire

1. In her study on Nicaraguan revolution, Ileana Rodríguez proposes that the revolutionary state's rhetoric is articulated with a masculine "I" that "obstructs democratic representation" (xv). A similar assimilation of the masculine into the discourse of revolutionary nation is found in Mexican Revolution.
2. For a longer documentation and discussions on these polemics, see Víctor Díaz Arciniega (1989), Guillermo Sheridan (1993 and 1999), Daniel Balderston (1998), and Mary K. Long (1995).
3. Robert M. Irwin notes—following the suggestion of Carlos Monsiváis—that there was a Freudization of the country in the beginning of twentieth century—that homophobia in Mexico was possible because of the influence of psychoanalysis (Irwin 1998, 32). In an earlier work, while writing about Salvador Novo's autobiography, I have pointed out psychoanalysis allows the homosexual subject to know himself as homosexual, that is to know himself through pathology. It was necessary to pass through the episteme of pathology to gain self-knowledge, as if the definition of homosexuality entailed the precondition of self-imposed homophobia (Domínguez 2001, 137–138). Antonio Marquet, on the other hand, suggests that "even though Novo rejects psychoanalysis considering it a 'harmful attempt [at explanation],' he uses psychoanalytic jargon and refers to it very often, which empowers him, since it arms him with knowledge, experience, and a lexicon that allows him to organize his remembrances within an explanatory logic, to rebuild them, and finally to invent them" (47). The pathological discourse is therefore one of the main supports for knowing homosexuality and it becomes the condition for its appearance in the public sphere.
4. In her book *A Queer Mother for the Nation: The State and Gabriela Mistral*, Licia Fiol-Matta notes that the masculinization of Gabriela Mistral was convenient for the educative project that Vasconcelos promoted, asserting that she was not feminine and that she represented a strong figure (9–10).

5   The Sentimental Men: Educating Machos in Mexican Cinema

1. Sergio de la Mora, in his work on the iconography of Pedro Infante, suggests that the strategies for the construction of masculinities are closely related to the rhetoric of the national (46–49).

2. In October 2003, the Museum Carrillo Gil in Mexico City showed the exhibition *Estética socialista en México: Siglo XX* [The Socialist Aesthetics in Mexico: Twentieth Century]. It focused on how socialist aesthetics influenced the formation of the national imaginary. In Mexican socialist art, the education of the masses and the exaltation of the "bronze" race (the Mexican version of the new man, proposed by José Vasconcelos in his *La raza cósmica*) are the two main topics. The iconography of the *Escuela mexicana de pintura* to which Orozco and Siqueiros belong features this bronze man as the mestizo who is the sacrificial victim and the violent subject at the same time. Thus, the *pathos* that defines the male image in this aesthetics consists of a paradox: a utopia of work and vitality is depicted with bloody bodies, victimized to the point of fatalism.

3. It is important to remember that parallel to the *comedia ranchera*, the films about prostitutes constitute another significant trend in the Mexican cinema. One leit motif of these films (as we can see in *Santa*, *La mujer del puerto*, etc.) is the deception and abandonment of naive girls from the countryside by seductive machos. In 1944—two years before *Los tres García*—*Las abandonadas* (directed by Emilio Fernández) was released. This film is one of the most significant pieces of melodrama about prostitutes and it also includes, as a point of departure for the woman's fate, the deception by a man. When Luis Antonio says, "They are the abandoned ones," he is probably referring to this film by Fernández.

4. This is the Mexican adaptation of the novel with same title by the Chilean writer José Domoso. It could be argued that this novel belongs to the Chilean tradition and for that reason it would not be the best example to illustrate an aspect of Mexican machismo. Nevertheless, adaptations and remakes made in Mexican cinema such as *La Perla* by Emilio Fernández, on the short story by the American writer Steinbeck and *Nazarín* by Luis Buñuel based on the novel by de Spaniard novelist Benito Pérez Galdós, among others, were produced bearing in mind the logic of the Mexican cinema market, which is that the same audience admired the revolutionary pictures, the *comedia ranchera*, and films about prostitution.

6   Building on the Negative: The Diagnosis of the Nation

1. For broader research regarding this period of the Mexican left, see Barry Carr's *La izquierda mexicana a través del siglo XX* [The Mexican Left through the Twentieth Century] and the novel by Carlos Montemayor *Los informes secretos* [The Secret Reports], in which we can see how the PRI's web of infiltration and violent actions against the clandestine left in Mexico effectively silenced socialist dissidence.

2. According to Massimo Modonessi, in his *La crisis histórica de la izquerda socialista mexicana* [The Historical Crisis of the Mexican Socialist Left], 1968 means a divide not only for the Mexican left but also for the history of the country at large, because the acts of oppression against the intellectual sector

brought to light, on the one hand, the obsolescence of the PRI and, on the other, the crisis of representation of the left, which, as José Revueltas had pointed out in his *Ensayo sobre un proletariado sin cabeza* [Essay on a Proletariat without Head], lacked power to influence society. A large critical oeuvre on machismo and national identity was produced in the context of a state project that started in Lázaro Cárdenas' regime but went into decay in the political crisis of 1968.

3. Here I agree with Emilio Bejel and Robert M. Irwin, who have referred earlier to the work of Doris Sommer as a point of departure for deconstructing patriarchal hegemony from the gendering-erotic basis of the nation. According to Bejel, "[B]ecause homosexuality constitutes an integral part, by negation, of the narrative proposed by the national romances, it continually threatens to destabilize those very romances" (xvi). Irwin observes that Sommer, by stating that heterosexual relationships are allegories of the national integration, "neglects to explore a parallel allegorical strategy for constructing nationhood: male homosocial bonding" (Irwin 2003, xxvii). Both authors depart from the criticism of heterosexual norms; for them, if the nation is constructed on the basis of a heterosexual norm in a patriarchal system, it is inside masculine culture (codes, meanings, imaginaries) where we can find the kernel of its destabilization, that is, its dialectical negation.

4. It is not the writers of the first half of twentieth century alone who focus on the macho figure. The ethnographers who have studied Mexican culture throughout the century have also produced a number of significant works that have contributed to the development of this criticique of machismo. To name a few, Américo Paredes' work on Mexican-American corridos, Oscar Lewis' on poverty and family structure in Mexico City, Matthew Guttmann's on daily life of urban, low- and middle-class men, Joseph Carrier's, Guillermo Núñez's and Annick Prieur's on homoeroticisms, Marina Castañeda's therapy reports on the invisible machismo and Fernando Huerta's on soccer teams form part of a larger archive that focuses on the image of macho.

5. "The pealed one" would be the literal translation of *pelado*. *Pelado* means "naked" in the Mexican dialect, connoting a precarious condition. Because of its difficult translation I prefer to leave it in Spanish.

6. The term "ladino" connotes a reserved and treacherous personality and is applied to Indians who speak Spanish or mestizos.

7. For a broad view of this literature, see Mario Muñoz (1996), Mario Schneider (1997), and Antonio Marquet (2001).

8. I use abjection as defined by Kristeva: the condition of being the object of no desire (1–2).

7   Inferiority and Rancor: The Fearful Mestizo

1. In her *Travestismos culturales: literatura y etnografía en Cuba y Brasil*, Jossianna Arroyo points out the hegemonic idea of mestizo as harmonious "panacea" of identity discourse in Latin America (11–12). Following Cornejo

Polar assertions on conflictive constitution of race in the region, Arroyo offers an explanation of the contradictions of sensuality and oppression in the representations of black population in Cuba and Brazil.

2. The expression "imagined community" refers to the definition of nation by Benedict Anderson. I use this terminology in order to underscore the link between man and nation that has been one of the axes of this book.

3. In the background of the frivolity that entertains the middle class in the 1960s, notes Carlos Monsiváis, the coercion of the PRI was relentless against dissidents. Practically all literature that alludes to the PRI regime has suggested this double phase of paternalism and intolerant coercion. The algid point of this criticism is the abundant literature written about the massacre of students in 1968 during the regime of Gustavo Díaz Ordaz.

4. I have alluded to this macho homoeroticism when discussing Octavio Paz's *El laberitno de la soledad*, and will insist on it again in the next chapter. Bruno Bert, in his essay "La lengua de la serpiente: acerca de la crítica social de la doble moral" [The serpent's tongue: on the social criticism of the double standard"] has also pointed out this aspect in *Los gallos salvajes* (39).

8   Mayate: The Queerest Queer

1. In addition to the novels mentioned in this chapter, we can refer to the preference of Salvador Novo for bus drivers and soldiers (*La estatua de sal*), Xavier Villaurrutia's preference for shoe-shines (Aguilar *Una vida no-velada*), and ethnographic works by Joseph Carrier, Annick Prieur, and Patricia Ponce, among others.

2. MacCannell defines "cultural experience" as follows: "[T]he data of cultural experiences are somewhat fictionalised, idealised or exaggerated models of social life that are in the public domain, in film, fiction, political rhetoric, small talk, comic strips . . . all tourist attractions are cultural experiences" (cit. in Sánchez Taylor 41).

Bibliography

Anzaldo, Demetrio. "*Las púberes canéforas*, la sensibilidad social y sexual en la nocturna Ciudad de México." *Ciberletras*. Accessed on June 16, 2007. www.lehman.cuny.edu/ciberletras/v11/anzaldo.html

Arendt, Hanna. *The Origins of Totalitarism*. New York-London: Harcourt Brace & Company, 1976.

Argüelles, Hugo. *Trilogía de los ritos: La Galería del silencio, El ritual de la salamandra, Escarabajos*. México: Plaza y Valdés, 1997.

——. *Obras*. México: Grupo Editorial Gaceta, 1994, vol. 1.

——. *Trilogía musical*. Toluca: Universidad Autónoma del Estado de México, 1994, vol. 2.

Arroyo-Martínez, Jossianna. *Transvestismos culturales*. Pittsburgh: Instituto Internacional de Literatura Iberoamericana, 2003.

Bakhtin, Mijail. *Estética de la cración verbal*. Trans. Tatiana Bubnova. México: Siglo XXI, 1982.

Balderston, Daniel. "Poetry, Revolution, Homophobia: Polemics from the Mexican Revolution." In Sylvia Molloy and Robert McKee Irwin, eds. *Hispanism and Homosexualities*. Durham: Duke University Press, 1998.

Barthes, Roland. *Mitologías*. Mexico: Siglo XXI, 1986.

Bartra, Roger. *Oficio mexicano*. México: CONACULTA, 2003.

Baudrillard, Jean. *De la seducción*. Trans. Elena Banarroch. México: Red Editorial Iberoamericana, 1990.

Bautista, Juan Carlos, dir. *Amor Chacal*. México: Producciones Pily y Mili, 2001.

Bejel, Emilio. *Gay Cuban Nation*. Chicago: University of Chicago Press, 2001.

Benítez Rohry, Adriana Candia, Patricia Cabrera, Guadalupe de la Mora, Josefina Martínez, Isabel Velázquez, and Ramona Ortiz. *El silencio que la voz de todas quiebra*. Chihuahua: Azar, 1999.

Bert, Bruno. "La lengua de la serpiente: acerca de la crítica social a la doble moral." In Edgar Ceballos, ed. *Hugo Argüelles. Estilo y dramaturgia*. México: INBA-Gaceta, 1994.

Bhabha, Homi K. "DissemiNation: Time, Narrative, and the Margins of the Modern Nation." In Homi K. Bhabha, ed. *Nation and Narration*. London-New York: Routledge, 1990.

Blanco, José Joaquín. *Función de medianoche*. México: Era, 1981.

——. *Las púberes canéforas*. México: Océano, 1983.

Bleys, Rudy C. *Images of Ambiente. Homosexuality and Latin American Art 1810–Today*. London-New York: Continuum, 2000.

Bonfil, Carlos, and Carlos Monsiváis. *A través del espejo. El cine mexicano y su público*. México: Ediciones El Milagro, Instituto Mexicano de Cinematografía, 1994.

Bordo, Susan. *The Male Body. A New Look at Men in Public and in Private*. New York: Farrar, Straus, and Giroux, 1999.

Boswell, John. *Christianity, Social Tolerance, and Homosexuality*. Chicago: University of Chicago Press, 1980.

Bourdieu, Pierre. *Distinction. A Social Critique of the Judgement of Taste*. Trans. Richard Nice. Cambridge: Harvard University Press, 1984.

———. *La dominación masculina*. Barcelona: Anagrama, 2000.

———. *The Logic of Practice*. Trans. Richard Nice. Stanford: Stanford University Press, 1990.

Buffington, Robert. "Homophobia and the Mexican Working Class, 1900–1910." In Robert M. Irwin, Edward J. McCaughan, and Michelle Rocío Nasser, eds. *The Famous 41. Sexuality and Social Control in Mexico, c.1901*. New York: Palgrave Macmillan, 2003, 193–225.

Butler, Judith. *Bodies that Matter*. New York: Routledge, 1993.

———. *Excitable Speech. A Politics of the Performative*. New York: Routledge, 1997.

Carr, Barry. *La izquierda mexicana a través del siglo XX*. México: Era, 1996.

Castañeda, Marina. *El machismo invisible*. México: Grijalbo, 2002.

Ceballos Maldonado, José. *Después de todo*. México: Premiá, 1986 (1969).

Certeau, Michel de. *La invención de lo cotidiano*. México: Universidad Iberoamericana, 1996.

Chacón, Tomás. *Cuentas pendientes*. Ciudad Juárez: H. Ayuntamiento de Juárez/ Escuela Superior de Agricultura, 1992.

Charlot, Jean. "Manuel Manilla, grabador mexicano." In Mercurio López Casillas, ed. *Monografía de 598 estampas de Manuel Manilla, grabador mexicano*. México: RM, 2005.

Conde, Teresa del. *Historia mínima del arte mexicano del siglo XX*. Mexico: ATAME, 1994.

Connell, R.W. *Masculinidades*. Trans. Irene Ma. Artigas. México: PUEG-UNAM, 1993.

Cordero Reiman, Carmen. "Introduction." *El cuerpo aludido: anatomías y construcciones*. Catalogue. Mexico: Instituto Nacional de Bellas Artes, 1998.

Covarrubias, Alicia. "El vampiro de la colonia Roma de Luis Zapata: la nueva picaresca y el reportaje ficticio." *Revista de crítica literaria latinoamericana* 20:39 (Spring–Summer 1994): 183–197.

Deleuze, Guilles. *Coldmess and Cruelty*. Trans. Jean McNeil. New York: Zone Books, 1991.

Deleuze, Gilles, and Felix Guattari. *El antiedipo. Capitalismo y esquizofrenia*. Trans. Francisco Monge. México: Paidós, 1995.

Derrida, Jaques. *A Derrida Reader: Between the Blinds*. New York: Columbia University Press, 1991.

Díaz Arciniega, Víctor. *Querella por la cultura "revolucionaria" (1925)*. México: Fondo de Cultura Económica, 1989.

Domínguez Ruvalcaba, Héctor. *La modernidad abyecta: Formación del discurso homosexual en Hispanoamérica*. Xalapa: Universidad Veracruzana 2001.

❧ Fiol-Mata, Licia. *A Queer Mother for the Nation: The State and Gabriela Mistral*. Minneapolis: University of Minnesota Press, 2002.

Foucault, Michel. *Historia de la sexualidad. 1-La voluntad de saber*. Trans. Ulises Guiñazú. México: Siglo XXI, 1982.

Fromm Erich, and Michael Maccoby. *Sociopsicoanálisis del campesino mexicano: Estudio de la economía y la psicología de una comunidad rural*. México: Fondo de Cultura Económica, 1979.

Gamboa, Federico. *Del natural*. México: Eusebio Gómez de la Puente, 1915.

Garber, Marjorie. *Bisexuality and the Eroticism of Everyday Life*. New York: Routledge, 2000.

García Canclini, Néstor. *Culturas híbridas: Estrategias para entrar y salir de la modernidad*. México: Grijalbo-CONACULTA, 1990.

————. *Consumidores y ciudadanos: Conflictos multiculturales de la globalización*. Mexico: Grijalbo, 1995.

Girard, René. *Mentira romántica y verdad novelesca*. Trans. Joaquín Jordá. Barcelona: Anagrama, 1985 (1961).

González Rodríguez, Sergio. *Huesos en el desierto*. Barcelona: Anagrama, 2002.

Guzmán, Martín Luis. *El águila y la serpiente*. Madrid: Compañía Iberoamericana de Publicaciones, 1928.

————. *Memorias de Pancho Villa*. México: Compañía General de Ediciones, 1960.

Hans, James S. *The Site of Our Lives: The Self and the Subject from Emerson to Foucault*. New York: University of New York Press, 1995.

Heller, Agnes. *Historia y vida cotidiana. Aportación a la sociología socialista*. Tran. M. Sacristán. México: Grijalbo, 1985.

Hernández Flores, Jorge. "El fin del mito presidencial." In Enrique Florescano, ed. *Mitos mexicanos*. México: Aguilar-Taurus-Alfaguara, 1995, 37–44.

Irwin, Robert M. *Mexican Masculinities*. Minneapolis: University of Minnesota Press, 2003.

————. "The Legend of Jorge Cuesta: the Peril of Alchemy and the Paranoia of Gender." In Sylvia Molloy and Robert M. Irwin, eds. *Hispanisms and Homosexualities*. Durham-London: Duke University Press, 1998.

Irwin, Robert M., Edward J. McCaughan, and Michelle Rocío Nasser. "Introduction. Sexuality and Social Control in Mexico, 1901." In Robert M. Irwin, Edward J. McCaughan and Michelle Rocío Nasser, eds. *The Famous 41. Sexuality and Social Control in Mexico, c.1901*. New York: Palgrave Macmillan, 2003, 1–18.

Kant, Immanuel. *Critique of Judgement*. Trans. J.H. Bernard. London: Macmillan, 1914.

————. *Lo bello y lo sublime: La paz perpetua*. Trans. A. Sánchez Rivero and F. Rivera Pastor. Madrid: Espasa-Calpe, 1982.

174   Bibliography

Kimmel, Michael S. "Homofobia, temor, vergüenza y silencio en la identidad masculina." In Teresa Valdés and José Olavarría, eds. *Masculinidad/es. Poder y crisis*. Santiago: Isis Internacional-FLACSO, 1997.

Kristeva, Julia. *Powers of Horror. An Essay on Abjection*. New York: Columbia University Press, 1982.

Lacan, Jacques. *Escritos*. Trans. Tomás Segovia. México: Siglo XXI, 1984.

Lagarde, Marcela. *Los cautiverios de las mujeres: madresposas, monjas, putas, presas y locas*. México: UNAM, 1990.

Larrain, Jorge. *Identidad y modernidad en América Latina*. México: Océano, 2000.

Lauretis, Teresa de. *Technologies of Gender: Essays on Theory, Film, and Fiction*. Bloomington: Indiana University Press, 1987.

Lazarus. Neil. *Nationalism and Cultural Practice in the Postcolonial World*. Cambridge: Cambridge University Press, 1999.

Levinas, Emmanuel. *La huella del otro*. Trans. Ester Cohen, Silvana Rabinovich, and Manrico Montero. México: Taurus, 2000.

Long, Mary Kendall. "Salvador Novo: 1920–1940, between the Avant-garde and the Nation." Dissertation, Princeton University, 1995.

López, Oscar. "*El vampiro de la colonia Roma o el travestismo posmoderno.*" *Revista de Literatura Mexicana Contemporánea* 4:10 (April–July 1999): 72–78.

López Velarde, Ramón. *Obras*. Mexico: Fondo de Cultura Económica, 1986.

Macías-González, Víctor. "The *Lagartijo* at *The High Life*. Masculine Consumption, Race, Nation, and Homosexuality in Porfirian Mexico." In Robert M. Irwin, Edward J. McCaughan, and Michelle Rocío Nasser, eds. *The Famous 41. Sexuality and Social Control in Mexico, c.1901*. New York: Palgrave Macmillan, 2003, 227–249.

Marquet, Antonio. *¡Que se quede el infinito sin estrellas!* México: Universidad Autónoma Metropolitana, 2001.

Martín-Barbero, Jesús. *Al sur de la modernidad*. Pittsburgh: Instituto Internacional de Literatura Iberoamericana, 2001.

Modonesi, Massimo. *La crisis histórica de la izquerda socialista mexicana*. México: Casa Juan Pablos-Universidad e la Ciudad de México, 2003.

Monsiváis, Carlos. *Amor perdido*. México: Era, 1977.

———. "Prólogo." In Salvador Novo. *Estatua de sal*. México: CONACULTA, 1998.

———. *Yo te bendigo, vida. Amado Nervo: crónica de vida y obra*. Tepic: Gobierno del Estado de Nayarit, 2002.

Montaldo, Graciela. *La sensibilidad amenazada: Fin de siglo y modernismo*. Rosario, Argentina: Beatriz Viterbo Editora, 1994.

Montemayor, Carlos. *Los informes secretos*. México: Joaquín Mortiz, 1999.

Mora, Sergio de la. "Masculinidad y mexicanidad: panorama teórico-bibliográfico." In Julianne Burton-Carvajal and Patricia Torres, eds. *Horizontes del segundo siglo: investigación pedagogía del cine mexicano, latinoamericano y chicano*. Guadalajara-México: Universidad de Guadalajara-Instituto Mexicano de Cinematografía, 1998.

Muñiz, Elsa. *Cuerpo, representación y poder. México en los albores de la reconstrucción nacional, 1920–1934.* México: Universidad Autónoma Metropolitana-Miguel Ángel Porrúa, 2002.

Muñoz, Mario. "Prólogo." In Mario Muñoz, ed. *De amores marginales: 16 cuentos mexicanos.* Xalapa: Universidad Veracruzana, 1996.

Nervo, Amado. *Obras completas.* Madrid: Aguilar, 1973.

Novo, Salvador. *Sátira. El libro ca . . .* México: Diana, 1978.

Núñez Noriega, Guillermo. *Sexo entre varones: Poder y resistencia en el campo sexual.* México: Miguel Ángel Porrúa-El Colegio de Sonora-UNAM, 1999.

Odier, Charles. *La angustia y el pensamiento mágico. Ensayo de análisis psicogenético aplicado a la fobia y a la neurosis de abandono.* México: Fondo de Cultura Económica, 1961.

Ortiz, Bladimir. "Prostitución y homosexualidad: interpelaciones desde el margen en *El vampiro de la colonia Roma* de Luis Zapata." *Revista Iberoamericana* 65: 187 (April–June 1999): 327–339.

Paredes, Américo. "The United States, Mexico, and Machismo." *Journal of the Folklore Institute* 8 (1971): 17–37.

Paz, Octavio. *El laberinto de las soledad.* México: Fondo de Cultura Económica, 1959 (2nd edition, revised and updated).

———. *El ogro filantrópico. Historia y política 1971–1978.* México: Seix Barral, 1979.

Pérez, Francisco R. "El infierno social y personal del marginado: el homosexual en la Ciudad de México." *CLA* 41:2 (December 1997): 204–112.

Piccato, Pablo. "Interpretations of Sexuality in Mexico City Prisons." In Robert M. Irwin, Edward J. McCaughan, and Michelle Rocío Nasser, eds. *The Famous 41: Sexuality and Social Control in Mexico, c.1901.* New York: Palgrave Macmillan, 2003, 261–266.

Ponce, Patricia. "Sexualidades costeñas." *Desacatos. Revista de Atropología Social* 6 (Spring–Summer 2001): 111–136.

Prieur, Annick. *Mema's House, on Transvestites, Queens, and Machos.* Chicago: University of Chicago Press, 1998.

Rama, Ángel. *Las máscaras democráticas del modernismo.* Montevideo: Fundación Ángel Rama, 1985.

Ramos, Julio. *Desencuentros de la modernidad en América Latina.* México: Fondo de Cultura Económica, 1989.

Ramos, Samuel. *Perfil del hombre y la cultura en México.* México: SEP, 1987.

Revueltas, José. *Cuestionamientos e intenciones.* México: Era, 1978.

———. *Ensayo sobre un proletariado sin cabeza.* México: Era, 1980.

———. *Las evocaciones requeridas I.* México: Era, 1987.

———. *Los días terrenales.* México: Era, 1985.

———. *México: una democracia bárbara.* México: Era, 1983.

———. *Visión del Paricutín (y otras crónicas y reseñas).* México: Era, 1983.

Reyes, Alfonso. *Notas sobre la inteligencia americana.* México: UNAM, 1978.

Rian, Chris, and C. Michael Hall. *Sex Tourism: Marginal People and Liminalities.* London-New York: Routledge, 2001.

Richard, N. *Masculino/femenino: prácticas de la diferencia y cultura democrática.* Santiago: Francisco Zeger, 1993.

Rodríguez, Ileana. *Women, Guerrillas and Love: Understanding War in Central America.* Minneapolis: University of Minnesota Press, 1996.

Romero, Rubén José. "Apuntes de un lugareño." In Antonio Castro Leal, ed. *La novela de la revolución mexicana.* México: Aguilar, 1964.

———. "Desbandada." In Antonio Castro Leal, ed. *La novela de la revolución mexicana.* México: Aguilar, 1964.

Romero de Terreros, Manuel. *Catálogos de las exposiciones de la antigua academia de San Carlos de México, 1850–1898.* México: Imprenta Universitaria, 1963.

Ronquillo, Victor. *Las muertas de Juarez: cronica de una larga pesadilla.* México, D.F.: Planeta Mexicana, 1999.

Rubin, Gayle. "El tráfico de mujeres: notas sobre la economía política del sexo." *Nueva antropología* 30 (November 1986): 95–145.

Sánchez-Taylor, Jacqueline. "Tourism and 'Embodied' Commodities: Sex Tourism in the Caribbean." In Stephen Clift and Simon Carter, eds. *Tourism and Sex: Culture, Commerce and Coercion.* Chicago: University of Chicago Press, 2000.

Sarlo, Beatriz. *Una modernidad periférica: Buenos Aires 1920 y 1930.* Buenos Aires: Nueva Visión, 1999.

Schneider, Luis Mario. *La novela mexicana entre el petróleo, la homosexualidad y la política.* México: Nueva Imagen, 1997.

Seidler, Victor J. *Rediscovering Masculinity: Reason, Language and Sexuality.* London-New York: Routledge, 1989.

Sheridan, Guillermo. *México en 1932: la polémica nacionalista.* México: Fondo de Cultura Económica, 1999.

Sommer, Doris. *Foundational Fictions. The National Romances of Latin America.* Berkeley: University of California Press, 1993.

Spivak, Gayatri Chakravorty. "Can the Subaltern Speak?" In Patrick Williams and Laura Chrisman, eds. *Colonial Discourse and Post-Colonial Theory. A Reader.* New York: Columbia University Press, 1994.

Stavenhagen, Rodolfo. *La cuestión étnica.* México: El Colegio de México, 2001.

Talavera Trejo, Manuel. *Novenario.* Chihuahua: Universidad Autónoma de Chihuahua, 1994.

Toussaint, Manuel. *Saturnino Herrán y su obra.* México: UNAM-Instituto de Cultura de Aguascalientes-INBA, 1990.

Urbina, Luis G. "El baño del centauro." In José Emilio Pacheco, ed. *Antología del modernismo (1884–1921).* México: UNAM, 1999.

Urquizo, Francisco L. *Tropa vieja.* In Antonio Castro Leal, ed. *La novela de la revolución mexicana.* México: Aguilar, 1964.

Velazquez Martínez del Campo, Roxana. "De la academia al porfiriato." In Magdalena Zavala and Alejandrina Escudero, eds. *Escultura mexicana. De la Academia a la instalación.* México: CONACULTA-INBA-Américo Arte, 2001.

Viñas Moisés. *Historia del cine mexicano.* México: UNAM-UNESCO, 1987.

Zapata, Luis. *El vampiro de la Colonia Roma*. México: Grijalbo, 1979.

Žižek, Slavoj. *Tarrying with the Negative: Kant, Hegel, and the Critique of Ideology*. Durham: Duke University Press, 1993.

———. *The Metastases of Enjoyment: Six Essays on Woman Causality*. New York: Verso, 1994.

Zúñiga, Antonio. *El gol de oro (el puchador)*. Tijuana: CAEN editores, 1999.

———. "Estrella enterradas." *El armario. Suplemento cultural semanal 50. El semanario* 12: 517 (February 19, 2001): 22–32.

Index

CPSIA information can be obtained
at www.ICGtesting.com
Printed in the USA
LVHW050006300519
619460LV00014B/795/P